Throw the Rabbit is your passport to greater sales and success. You will be introduced to high-impact sales ideas that will turbo-charge your sales career beginning today. Joe Bonura's unique hands-on approach to the sales process is written from his forty-year "library of life" experiences. Every year, Joe invests over two hundred hours in the real world of selling, making real sales calls with real sales people (or as Joe calls them - Serve People). His client list includes Sony Corporation, Atlas Van Lines, and Blue Cross/Blue Shield, plus hundreds of other businesses.

You will learn:

✔ How to "Throw the Rabbit" on every sales call

✔ How to re-ignite, relight, and re-excite your enthusiasm for selling

✔ How to master the three-dimensions of a sales call

✔ How to become a telemaster© instead of a telemarketer

✔ How to empower yourself to empower your customers

✔ How to use the perfect sales process for greater success

✔ How to turn objections into reasons to buy

✔ How to use the only way to close a sale

And many more revenue-generating ideas that will help you out-think, out-perform, out-service, and out-sell the competition.

D1306989

Throw the Rabbit©

The Ultimate Approach To Three-Dimensional Selling©

Joe Bonura, CSP

WARDMAN PARK
PUBLISHING

Throw The Rabbit...The Ultimate Approach to Three-Dimensional Selling

ISBN: 0-9661707-2-5

E-mail Joe Bonura: joe@bonura.com

To order additional copies of this title,
call 800-444-3340 or visit
website: www.bonura.com

Photography by Nick Bonura
Illustrations by Steve Logsdon

This book is dedicated to my wife

Carol

She has always walked before me, behind me, and alongside me, encircling me with her love and support for the past 40 years.

Foreword

You will not find any sales theory in *Throw the Rabbit*. You will find a dynamic and energetic approach that creates powerful sales results. Joe Bonura has written a sales book that will have a major impact on your sales career and the careers of sales people across the country. This book is not just another take on sales basics rewritten for the hundredth time. It has been written by a veteran sales person who has spent his life in the profession that we all love to love—Sales.

Joe's forty years of experience in sales and marketing have produced a reliable and convincing approach to becoming a sales superstar in any industry. It is easy to learn and it requires only a personal commitment to adopt new habits and a sincere desire to see your customers achieve successful outcomes in their lives.

I truly believe that Joe has something here. Joe gives us fundamentally sound sales principles that work, and his illustrations are marvelous applications of those principles. We see fine examples of each step of the sales process, nothing left out, with a motivating theme that circulates throughout.

Joe makes selling easy; from his genuinely friendly style to his professional and creative techniques, we get the entire sales picture from the first contact, to the sale, and to repeat sales.

Joe's philosophy is to view his possibilities as unlimited— no boundaries! Whether you are selling a product or a service, this book will take you to the next level of your sales career and beyond. I know that you will enjoy reading a book written from the library of Joe's life.

Zig Ziglar

Contents

Throw the Rabbit

The Ultimate Approach to Three-Dimensional Selling©

Joe Bonura, CSP

Acknowledgments

So many people have contributed to my success and to the completion of this book that it is hard to know where to begin. I would like to thank my father, Joe Bonura, Jr., for the inspiration he gave me to seek a sales career, and my mother, Rosemary Bonura, who is the ultimate serve person. I thank my wife Carol and my daughter Ann Carol Yoho, who have made my speaking words make sense on paper. My sisters Linda Cook and Kay Bollinger were always present with a word of encouragement. Joe and Nick, two of the best sons any man could ask for, live what I teach in this book, and their personal successes prove it.

I am indebted to the three great friends and role models, who gave me my first break in sales: Clark Harvey former sales manager at WNOE Radio in New Orleans, the late Ed Martin of General Electric Company, and Ed Fessel, past president of Fessel, Siegfriedt, & Moeller Advertising Agency.

I also remember the sales and motivational giants, who gave me inspiration through books, recordings, and seminars when I most needed it: Earl Nightingale, Dale Carnegie, and Zig Ziglar.

Next on my list are the friends who guided and encouraged me to change the direction of my life and move into the world of professional speaking: Elizabeth Jeffries, Ty Boyd, and Cavett Robert.

I am grateful to Terre Bryant, my marketing director, who organized and booked my speaking engagements while I concentrated on the contents of this book.

This book has taken over forty years to write. It is impossible to list everyone who has made it possible, but my gratitude to you is immense because without your input, inspiration, and help, this book would not have been written.

Introduction

There are select few sales people who win the awards, who get the repeat business, who earn the big salaries. Would you like to be one of them? After studying hundreds of sales people in the field, and being one of them, Joe Bonura discovered the secret to being a sales success. He will share how to apply that secret to your selling habits so that you can earn more money in selling by serving more people. Observe carefully what Joe has found to be the key.

Sales superstars see selling three-dimensionally by viewing the whole picture of the sales process and developing the entire business relationship. Building relationships is important in successful selling. Would you like to know how to sell more products and services to new and existing clients, or how to get through the gatekeeper on a cold call, or how to win an account with a big corporation? Joe will show you how with three-dimensional selling. By reading this book, you will learn how to maneuver your way to a sale. You will discover how to transform others' perceptions of you from a mere sales rep to a welcomed problem solver.

Perhaps you are at home now or in your office thinking, "So what? What is in it for me?" Once you learn to be a problem solver and see selling three-dimensionally, you will sell more in less time, and that means more family time, more leisure time, more recreational time. You will enjoy spending the additional money you will be making.

Why should you listen to Joe Bonura, and what makes him the expert? As a professional speaker, trainer, and consultant, Joe has taught people all over the world to increase sales and to improve service. His real-world approach has been applied to many of his clients, among them: Atlas Van Lines, Sony Electronics, Lexmark, and Blue Cross/Blue Shield.

Chapter 1
Throw the Rabbit

Do you remember your first sales call? In 1964, I made my first sales call as a radio sales rep for WNOE Radio in New Orleans. My sales training had consisted of my boss introducing me to several of the station's existing clients. That was it! After that, he turned me loose and said, "OK, Joe, go for it!"

I drove my black Volkswagen Beetle to a furniture store in New Orleans, and I'll never forget it...it took me 10 minutes to get out of the car! I sat there because I was too frightened to get out!   Finally, I gathered my nerve, walked into the store, and stuttered to the receptionist, "Uh, is, uh, may I, uh, is Mr...."

Seeing my inexperience, she took pity on me and responded, "I will get him." The previous evening, I had read a sales book that advised sales people to begin with a compliment. When I noticed a large swordfish on the wall, I figured that would work. A large, gruff-looking man approached me as I introduced myself and applied the prepared compliment, "H..hi, my name is Joe Bonura. D..did you catch that big fish?"

He did not "bite" at my compliment, and he rudely replied, "And what are you selling?"

I replied meekly, "WNOE Radio."

He bellowed, "Well, I do not want any!"

"OK, here is my card. Thank you very much." I turned around, ran out of the store, and mentally quit my new sales career. No way was I going to do this for a living, and subject myself to abuse.

It was February in New Orleans, with the Easter season approaching, and I was lugging around a six-foot Easter rabbit in my Volkswagen passenger seat. If the customer purchased a thirteen-week radio schedule, the rabbit went with the package. I was very nervous, and I had forgotten to use the rabbit on the first call. I knew I could not return to the station with the rabbit; that would concede to failure and defeat. So I decided to try one more time. I went where any new sales person would go - familiar territory! I went to my local Dorignac's Supermarket, where my wife and I shopped every week. I grabbed the six-foot Easter rabbit and entered the store, but the store checkers, who looked so nice last week when I was the customer, looked so intimidating this week.

When I asked for Mr. Dorignac, one of the checkers pointed to the little deli/restaurant where Mr. Dorignac was drinking coffee and observing the employees as they worked. When I nervously turned in his direction, I tripped, and the giant Easter rabbit flew into the air, crashed into a line of metal garbage cans, creating a domino effect, knocking over can after can. I was down on one knee, glanced up, and saw Mr. Dorignac sporting a huge grin. As I greeted him, he laughed and said, "Son, that is the best attention-getting technique in selling I have ever seen."

Well, I left the store with a contract for a 13-week radio schedule, and Mr. Dorignac had a successful promotion along with a huge, six-foot Easter rabbit, and I decided to give my sales career another chance. The lessons that I learned that day are used in my sales seminars, and **I call the process of being unique, Throwing the Rabbit.** It is not necessary to carry a giant Easter rabbit and trip over yourself to get a signed contract; however, if you want to stand out from your competition, you must be unique. There are many ways to "Throw the Rabbit," which I will share with you in this book.

Chapter 2
Turn Every Day Into Gold

I have personally experienced the nervousness and failures that all sales people do. I have had many embarrassing moments, but if I had not continued to try, I would not have written this book. *Selling is about getting out there, being rejected, returning again and again, and not letting the rejection stop you.* You have taken the initiative to purchase this book, so I will challenge you in four ways:

> **I will make you think. I will make you uncomfortable. I will make you the best YOU possible. I will show you how to turn every day into gold.**

Challenge #1: I will make you think and examine how you look at Sales. You will get many ideas to improve your skills— some old, some new. *Keep an open mind.* I do not want to make you think inside the box. I do not want to make you think outside the box. *I want you to get rid of the box.* You will expand the way you think about Sales, using no-limit boundaries to your mindset. This book will change some of your long-held views of the Sales profession, taking you far beyond Sales 101 and 102.

Challenge #2: I will make you uncomfortable with the status quo, where you are presently in your career, to a new level of achievement that you have never dreamed possible. The fact is: if you do not become uncomfortable with the new methods, you will not change from where you are to where you could be.

A good analogy of this is a story I tell about my little dog Muffin. When she was just a pup, I decided to crate train her. A trainer told me that a dog will not soil its own crate, so I locked Muffin in her crate each night and let her outside first thing every morning. For the first week, she cried and banged on the door of the crate, trying to get out. She quickly learned that the door was locked, and she could not get out.

One day the phone rang as I put Muffin in the crate, leaving the door closed, but not locked. When I finished my conversation, I headed for the supermarket. While shopping, I remembered that I had forgotten to lock the door on Muffin's crate. I hurried home, thinking that I would find Muffin destroying something, but to my amazement, she was in her crate, waiting for me to release her. She had learned not to try to get out of her crate. Sound familiar?

How many times in life, and in sales, have you knocked on a door only to find it locked? You eventually stopped trying and learned to stay safely inside your self-imposed boundary. This book will give you the tools to break out of your **comfort zone** to achieve all that you were meant to achieve. It will inspire and challenge you to turbo-charge your career.

Challenge #3: I will challenge you to develop the capabilities that are already inside of you. My purpose is *not* to create a Joe Bonura clone, selling and using *my* words, but to have you use your own style and personality. *You will become the best YOU possible.* Think of it like a smorgasbord: take a little from Zig Ziglar, a little from Jeffrey Gitomer, a little from Og

Mandino, a little from Joe Bonura, and a little from yourself and your own experiences to become the best you that you can possibly be. You are the sum total of the experiences you have had, the people you know, and the choices you make.

Your possibilities are unlimited, and my objective is to move your thinking and your actions in a positive direction.

Challenge #4: I will show you how to turn every day into gold. You will learn timesaving techniques and skill-building ideas to make every day productive and profitable. How often have you received good, helpful information from a seminar, but when you returned to the office, the phone rang, you put your seminar notes away, and three weeks later, they were forgotten? A year later, you blew the dust off the notes, and you could not read last year's scribbling.

Do not waste the time and money you invested in this book, but use the ideas and make them work. I have trained thousands of people who say the ideas work, but they work only if you implement them. *Turn your notes into action by applying the ideas into your own daily sales situations.*

Throwing the Rabbit

Be unique by accepting the four challenges, and you will turn every day into gold.

Chapter 3
Do You Suffer From IKTA?

In my live sales seminars, I display a hammer and ask an audience member what it is. The person responds that it is a hammer, and it hammers nails. I throw the hammer on the floor and tell it to hammer nails. But, will telling the hammer to nail, cause the hammer to work? Certainly not. Because it is simply a tool, you must lift the hammer to use it. My sales tools can revolutionize your sales process and help you increase your income. You will have a toolbox full of ideas, but *none of the tools will work unless you use them and apply them in your daily routine.*

> **None of the tools will work unless you use them and apply them in your daily routine.**

Now I have found many sales people who suffer from a serious sales virus called *IKTA*. It is spelled I-K-T-A. No, it is not something you get from a fish tank; that is *ick*. IKTA stands for I Know That Already. I will suggest some things, and you will think, "Come on, Joe, *I Know That Already*!" Yes, you may know it, but ARE YOU DOING IT? Knowledge alone is not power; knowledge becomes power when you use it. What matters is your response to what you know. When your subconscious says IKTA (*I know that already*), I want your conscious mind to ask, "But am I doing it?"

Throwing the Rabbit

Be conscious of your positive response to change and apply the tools that will make you effective in sales.

Chapter 4

From Sales Person to Serve Person

Now here is a significant question: What business are you in? Think about it for a minute and respond. What did you come up with? My seminar audiences have said, "I am in the retail business," or "I am in the banking business," or "I am in the advertising sales business." They are all correct answers, but I have a better one. Maybe you thought of it. You are in the problem-solving business. Your job, product, or service would not exist if there were no problems in business. Selling is about solving problems.

Think of it this way. Why does McDonald's exist? Because people get hungry. If people did not get hungry, they would not go to McDonald's, and McDonald's would be out of business. Why do you have a savings account? Because if you did not have a savings account, you would keep your money in a sock at home where someone could steal it, and more importantly, the money would not earn interest. In each example, there is a problem! Selling is solving people's problems. *You are in the business of satisfying needs and desires through solving problems.* What a great profession!

> **You are in the business of satisfying needs and desires through solving problems.**

Now that you have a new job description, change your job

title. When you solve customer problems, you are no longer a sales person; you are a *serve person*. That is S-E-R-V-E-P-E-R-S-O-N. Serve people make more money than sales people. If you *approach the marketplace and forget about being a sales person and start thinking of yourself as a serve person solving problems*, you will sell twice as much as any sales person.

Now I am not ashamed of the Sales profession, but selling has changed, and you must reposition yourself as one serving others' needs. When you are serving, you are not doing something TO clients; however, you are doing something FOR and WITH clients. They want to do business with you. But if you enter the sales process with the attitude that you are going to sell the client something, he is going to sense that you want his money in your pocket; whereas, if you help the customer, you are going to make more money automatically. When you enter a sales call with a servant attitude, the customer will know it.

> **When you enter a sales call with a servant attitude, the customer will know it**

Go back to your answer to the question, "What business are you in?" Write down a new answer based on how your product or service solves people's problems. Here are some examples. If you are a financial consultant, your answer might be, "I am in the business of helping people increase their investments." If you are an advertising sales rep, your answer might be, "I am in the business of helping retailers bring more shoppers into their stores." When people ask me the question, I say that I am in the business of helping people increase sales and improve customer service with real-world strategies. Next time you are at a social event or a business function and someone asks that question, try out your new answer and pay attention to the reaction you receive. I am sure it will be positive!

Throwing the Rabbit

Set yourself apart from the competition by serving rather than selling.

Chapter 5
The Most Important Person is You

Now before we proceed, we should discuss the most important person in the sales process. **You!** If you do not feel good about you, neither will your customers. No matter how many skills you have, you will not use them unless you feel good about yourself. The best way I know to help you become a better you is to tell you about the tough obstacles I had early in life and how I overcame them. I have been there, I know what it feels to be rejected. I know how important it is to change those negative feelings to become a successful sales person.

What gives me the credibility to tell you how to become successful? Well, you are reading a book by someone who was born in a housing project in New Orleans, Louisiana, who flunked the second grade, who was kicked out of the first high school he attended, who dropped out of college in his freshman year, and yet retired financially independent at 46 years old. Now that statement was not to impress you, but to emphasize the idea that if someone with my background can accomplish what I have, you can do the same.

I overcame feelings of low self-esteem that surfaced at a very young age. I did not fail the second grade like most kids, who go home for the summer and return to the same grade the following year. I did it the hard way, in mid-year. I went home from school one afternoon, and Mom and Dad broke the news, "Joey, we have some bad news. Beginning tomorrow, you are going back to the first grade."

Unconcerned until the next morning, I went to school and played with my friends until the bell rang to line up with my class. I lined up with my second grade friends. Now at this school, the first grade lined up next to the second grade, that lined up next to the third grade, and so forth on up to the eighth grade. When the second bell rang, and there was total silence, my second grade teacher pierced the silence with, "Joey, move to the first grade line; you are no longer in the second grade." So I stepped out of the line with the second graders and into line with the first graders. My second grade friends were not supportive. They called me, "Dummy," "Stupid," "Baby." My self-esteem was shattered, and I began to believe the labels they put on me.

I formed my low self-image that day and fell into a social coma. Forty years later, when I returned for my eighth-grade reunion, my classmates were surprised at the changes in me. I was not the same quiet Joey they remembered; they noticed a more confident and outgoing Joey when I gave the welcoming speech at the reunion. Because self-image creates who we are and how we feel about ourselves, we are the sum total of our experiences, the people we know, and the choices we make.

We are the sum total of our experiences, the people we know, and the choices we make.

In high school, I attended Cor Jesu, an all-male Catholic school. I said that I was quiet, but that does not mean that I was good. I remember sitting with my father in the principal's office, and the principal sternly pointing at me. He said "Mr. Bonura, please understand me, we do not want his kind in our high school." I will never forget the look on the principal's face and how inferior and debased I felt. I stuffed those negative feelings away, and I was happy to be leaving that difficult and disciplined environment.

Those high school memories and feelings resurfaced a few years ago, when I was invited by Trinity High School in Louisville, an all-male Catholic school, where my sons had graduated, to speak to the junior class about success in business. I related to the students that I was expelled from Cor Jesu. I told them that Trinity was a wonderful school, and they were getting an excellent education. After my presentation, Father Domhoff, a Trinity teacher, walked on stage with a bag filled with gifts for me. He presented a Trinity mug, tee-shirt, and school jacket, and I gratefully accepted them, realizing that my sons had prized the same items during their years at Trinity. But, the best gift of all was a framed object that read, "This diploma certifies that Joseph H. Bonura, III, is now a graduate of Trinity High School." Father Domhoff said, "You made it!" In front of one hundred young men, I experienced overwhelming emotion as I broke down and cried.

After all those years, being expelled from Cor Jesu still bothered me. Actually, I had stuffed the hurt deep inside of me. The Trinity award greatly affected me, and I continued to ponder its meaning, all the way home in my Lexus SC400. But what does that prove? It doesn't matter what car you drive, or how much money you have in the bank, or how big your house is. *What really matters is how you feel about the person inside of you?* That same principle is important in selling. If I could just inoculate sales people with that concept and get them to say, "Hey, I am special. I can do anything I want to do." If I could get you to believe that, then *there is not anything,* **not anything,** *that you cannot do.*

> **What really matters is how you feel about the person inside of you.**

I attended college and dropped out in my freshman year. I was married a year later and was working as a finance collector, the only job I could get with my background and education. Coincidentally, I was assigned to collect unpaid bills in the neighborhood where I was born. The neighborhood had become run down and dangerous. The police cautiously entered that neighborhood, and yet, I went armed with nothing but a pencil. Even though this was a thankless and sometimes dangerous occupation, it brought about a life-changing incident.

As I made my collections one day, I encountered a man who owed ten dollars to the finance company. When he invited me into his kitchen, I figured he was going to make some coffee, and then settle his account. Wrong! He pulled out a butcher knife and threatened, "Now, Mr. Bonura, what is it you are here to talk about?" Frightened, I responded, "Well, I am here to tell you that this month, I am going to pay your bill, but next month, you will have to pay it yourself." And then, I was gone. I ran out as fast as I could, thinking that job was not worth my life.

The following day, as I drove to work in my Volkswagen, I heard the deep, resonant voice of Earl Nightingale over the radio. He was the master of motivational recordings in the 60's. He was saying, "You can have, be, or do anything you want if you follow five simple principles." I was all ears when he outlined the five principles that changed my life.

> **You can have, be, or do anything you want if you follow five simple principles.**

Five Principles That Can Change Your Life

Imagine that your hand is a wagon wheel, and each finger is a spoke in that wheel, and each spoke represents a success principle. Like a wagon wheel, if any of the spokes (or success principles) are broken, the wheel is weak. So you cannot simply practice principles one, three, and four and be successful; you must follow all to get a positive impact for results in your personal life and in your sales career. The principles are as follows:

> BELIEVE
> FOCUS
> KNOWLEDGE
> PLAN
> ACTION

Believe and Achieve

Take **BELIEVE** as the starting principle that we will examine. The first thing I believe in is God because I could not accomplish anything without Him. After believing in God, I must believe in MYSELF. You must believe in YOURSELF.

Notice how a dog, with its tail between its legs, appears weak and incompetent. Sometimes our human body language gives the same signals to clients. *Your inside shows on the out-side.*

That reminds me of a story that conveys how self-image can affect your success. Many years ago, my wife Carol and I were vacationing in Puerto Rico, staying at the beautiful Dorado Beach Hotel, one of the finest in the area. One evening, hotel banquet manager Hendrick Santos had a cock-tail party for all his guests. As he took great pride in his hotel and the care of his guests, I asked him to tell me his success story, and what followed was an incredible account.

At sixteen years old, Hendrick Santos was a golf caddy at a fine hotel in Puerto Rico. He was invited to an awards ban-quet for the caddies; he was so poor that he had to borrow clothes to attend. As he stood in the lobby, waiting to enter the banquet, a prominent lady in the community approached him and asked if he was the manager. That moment changed his life because she planted the seed of hope that he could be a hotel manager some day. He could not sleep that night as he lay in bed visualizing that one day Hendrick Santos could be manager of a fine hotel in Puerto Rico. When he told his caddy friends, they laughed and told him not to waste his time think-ing about it because the manager position would be filled by someone from the States. Santos ignored the taunts of his friends; he was determined to accomplish his goal, and he did!

What did he have? Not money. Not experience. But belief in himself. Do you have that kind of belief in yourself?

Focus On Your Vision

What is your **FOCUS**? *If you do not focus on anything other than what you have, then you have already arrived.* Does that make sense? If you do not know where you are going, you are already there. If you are not going anywhere, you have already arrived, and there is nowhere else to go.

Once I conducted a seminar for graduating college students entitled, *How To Convert Your Education Into A Job.* When I asked an upcoming graduate what career he was pursuing, he replied that he was undecided. Questioning further, I asked what subjects he studied so I could guide him to potential careers, but he replied, "Oh, this and that." Then I asked him to choose any career he wanted, and he said he was not picky. His parents would have been wiser to take the $50,000 it cost to send him to college, put it in a trust account, and let him be a ditch digger! The point is that he had no focus. He didn't know where he was going. Where will he end up in life? He will probably become a professional student and get his Masters, Ph.D., and double DD. He will go to school for the rest of his life because he does not have a focus. What a waste!

In contrast, a female student, Shannon, was in the same seminar. She listened to the ideas that I shared about getting a job and making it happen. Excitedly, she told me later that day that she used the ideas to get an interview. What a contrast between the two students! Shannon had focus; she knew what she wanted. So, once she had the skills, she would be able to GO FOR IT!

When I was sixteen, I learned a lesson about focus from my father who was in the wholesale meat business. When my dad developed a strange lump on his nose, he went to the doctor for analysis. After several visits and five doctors, the consensus was surgery, and the next time I saw my dad, he had a bandage across his face where they had removed his nose. The diagnosis was rhabdo myo sarcoma. When we told a cousin who was a pathologist in Atlanta, he was so incredulous that he drove eight hours to New Orleans to view the cancer under the microscope. He told my Dad, who was only 39 years old, to get his papers in order; he had a rare and deadly form of cancer that was spreading rapidly. When I asked my Dad what we could do, he responded positively that he would continue to work on his goal of retiring at 55 years old. So we worked together that year and saw the business grow. When the lymph nodes on Dad's neck swelled, we knew what it was, and once again, the doctor recommended surgery. Well, I prayed hard and waited with my family for the results of the surgery that lasted for eight hours. The surgeon's prognosis was good and bad: Dad lost seven pints of blood, and we did not lose him; nevertheless, the cancer had returned. When I visited Dad a few days later, I was surprised when he slipped off the side of his bed, got into a boxing stance, and threw a few fake punches, and said, "Come on, Joey, let's go a round!"

I was skeptical and concerned and wondered how Dad viewed his future, and he repeated what he said before, that he would continue to work and build the business and look forward to retirement. He reached his goal, and today he is 84 years old and included in medical history for surviving the deadly cancer. He is in good health and walks every day. He beat the odds because he did not think about dying; he focused on living.

> **I learned how important it is to have a vision in the midst of adversity.**

Once I asked Dad how he reacted to his cancer when he was alone, and he answered, "Well, tell you what I did. I went to the Dairy Queen, bought myself a nice big shake, drove to the back of the lot, and when I started to drink the shake, I broke down and cried. Then I realized this crying would do me no good, so I decided to focus on living, and not on dying."

Where is your focus? Is it on the sales you did not make? Is it on the opportunities you missed? Life will take on a whole new flavor when you begin focusing on what you can do and on the sales you can close.

Take an action step now to help you focus. Before you make a sales call, write down your objectives, which may be simply to get the next appointment, or to determine the decision makers, or to get a commitment. Without an objective, you cannot gauge success. How will you know if you hit the mark when you have not defined the mark? Are you working for a paycheck, or are you working for a deeper reason?

> **Is your focus a paycheck or a purpose?**

When I landed my first job in advertising, I was so excited to be in the field of my dreams that I literally forgot payday. I was not working for money anymore; I was working because I enjoyed what I was doing.

Set an objective for your sales career and write it down. Once you do that, you will notice your progress. I might illustrate this concept with the purchase of my Mercedes SUV. Before I bought my SUV, I did not notice other Mercedes SUV's, but after I owned one, everyone had one! (They must have bought theirs after I bought mine.) Actually, I simply began noticing them because I had one. Apply that to selling. Once you have a focus for your sales career, you will notice opportunities you missed before. If your objective is to gain fifteen new clients in the Widget industry, begin noticing Widget advertisements in the newspaper. You might meet someone at a social event or business meeting who is president of a Widget Company. Everything falls into place when you have focus.

What You Don't Know Cannot Help You

Now we should discuss the third principle, **KNOWLEDGE**. If you are arrested today and accused of being a professional sales person, would they have enough evidence to convict you? Now here is one time in your life that you want to be guilty. Assume that you are on the witness stand, and the prosecuting attorney is going to ask you some questions. How will you answer them? Is you car tape player filled with the latest sales cassettes? Are your bookshelves lined with books authored by the hottest sales mentors? Does your calendar reveal that you have attended at least one educational seminar per quarter to perfect your craft? How many magazines on selling or on your profession do you subscribe to?

If you were found not guilty due to lack of evidence, you

need the third spoke in the wheel – Knowledge. One of the most important factors to becoming a professional in any field is to continue learning during your entire lifetime. Today, when information changes every millisecond, it is even more important that you continue your education.

I did not complete my story when I told you I dropped out of college and retired financially independent at 46 years old. When I returned to school, I was married and had responsibilities, and I realized how important it was to continue my education. My grades were excellent because the second time around, I knew my goals. I knew I wanted to own my own advertising agency, and I was excited to learn everything I could about advertising.

I attend the National Speakers Association conventions every year and meet the greats in speaking, like Zig Ziglar and Jeffrey Gitomer. When the masters and mature professionals attend the seminars in the audience, they too process the information and take notes. These professionals teach the speaking principles, and yet, they are not too grand to learn something new.

No matter how much you know, you can always learn something new.

I am not suggesting that you return to college to earn a Masters Degree in selling, but there are many ways to continue your life education. Set aside a daily reading time, perhaps waking earlier than usual to find time to study. I begin my day by reading something positive—the Bible. Then I read the local and national news and an industry magazine, like *Professional Speaker* or *Personal Selling Power*. Many times I will make sales calls that day, and Bingo! I have the opportunity to use something I learned that very morning.

> **When you receive new input, only then will you give new output.**

Perhaps you have stacks of things that you plan to read someday, but have not found the time. Gather all these items and put them in a special box or file labeled "To Read." Set aside a daily reading time and start with the first item in your reading box until your time is up.

One way to increase your sales knowledge is through, what my granddaughter's kindergarten teacher calls, "car learning." Mrs. Jackson recommends that parents quiz their children on math, spelling, and other subjects while riding in the car. Those short 15 to 20-minute rides are no longer downtime; they are learning time. Adults are not much different from kindergartners. Collect audiotapes or CD's on your industry, selling, personal development, anything that would make you a better professional. Pop them in for a 15-minute ride to work, a five-minute ride to lunch, and a 15-minute ride home. It all adds up to 35 minutes a day of car learning.

Do not fall into the trap that I fell into. When I wanted to speak Italian, I bought an audiocassette series on the subject; however, when that set did not work, I purchased another set. After purchasing seven sets on how to speak Italian, all I could say was *Buon Giorno*! If I had listened to and applied the first set, I would now be speaking another language. I was looking for the magic tape that promises you will be speaking the language of love in just a few short days. There is no magic tape; it takes sweat, practice, and hard work.

Another way to continue learning is to take a course or attend a seminar on Sales. There are a multitude of public seminar companies that hold open seminars in cities all over the country. Join an industry association and attend the educational seminar provided by the organization. One of the benefits of belonging to an industry association is the opportunity to receive customized education where they speak your sales language and know your product.

You might explore hiring a professional trainer to design a customized seminar for you or your company. Where do you find one? Your industry association is an excellent source for suggestions of professionals who know your industry. Contact me; my seminars have helped many clients get back on track with sales. I am also happy to recommend other trainers who can help you.

When my youngest son Nick graduated from the University of Dayton, I experienced firsthand the result of my investment in his education. While Nick held his diploma and I took his picture, several of his classmates passed and commented, "Well I can assure you that was the last book I will ever read!" Nick looked surprised and commented, "Gee, Dad, I thought that graduation was the beginning, not the end of our education." That comment was worth every penny that I invested in sending my son to college. He understood that education, like selling, is a process, and not an event.

> **Always view life as a beginning because the opportunity to learn is everywhere and ongoing.**

Considering all there is to learn about sales, how much do you know now? One-tenth of one percent? It is awesome to imagine how much knowledge there is to be attained if we have an open mind. Get started now; you have much to learn. The late Earl Nightingale, broadcaster and motivational guru, stated that if you spent just one hour a day studying any subject, within five years you would be an expert on that subject.

To make my point further, I mention Jim, a gentleman who had worked for a company for ten years, and the day came when the position he was seeking became available. He naturally assumed that he would be moved into that position. Dressed in his best suit, he entered the president's office expecting the promotion, only to be told that he was not a candidate for the position, and that the position would be given to John. Frustrated, he blurted, "What? You mean I have been with the company for ten years, and I am not getting the job? John has been here only five years." The president replied, "No, Jim, you have been with the company for one year times ten, while John has studied and learned new things about the job for five years."

Which category would you fall into? Have you spent the last ten years repeating what you learned in your first year on the job, or have you spent each year learning and growing in your profession? Now that the evidence is in, go back to my original question. If you were arrested today and accused of being a professional sales person, would they have enough evidence to convict you?

Do You Plan to Fail?

It is not a dumb question! Do you have a written **PLAN** for sales success? I said **written**, not a rough idea in your mind. If you do not have a formal plan on paper, then you plan to fail because *when you fail to plan, you plan to fail.* Your subconscious mind is like a heat-seeking missile, where once you find your focus and know where to aim, then you hit your target every time.

When Earl Nightingale recommended to formulate a plan, I thought about the field of advertising. In fact, I had written a newspaper advertising campaign for Volkswagen just for the fun of it, not thinking there might be a profession for me in advertising. I enjoyed watching television ads, and I created new and improved versions of the ads. At twenty years old, I wrote *Bon Advertising Agency* on a yellow legal pad, setting a goal to open my own advertising agency by the time I was thirty years old. I wrote to the American Association of Advertising Agencies for information on the advertising agency business. I had an artist to design a logo for future business cards and letterhead. That was it; I displayed the artwork where I could see it and imagine my goal as an actuality. Three months short of my thirtieth birthday, I opened Bon Advertising Agency, Incorporated. I knew my destiny because I had a plan and had boldly written it on paper. Bon Advertising became the second largest ad agency in the state of Kentucky and the third largest in the state of Louisiana.

What are your sales goals? What plans do you have to

develop your talents? What are your long-term goals ten years from now? Stop a minute and brainstorm, and write your dream list of selling goals. When you have completed your list, mark three goals you will accomplish this year. Take each of the top three goals and create a step-by-step tactical approach to accomplish each goal. Date and set deadlines for each approach. Now you have an achievable plan.

Action Power

A plan is worthless unless you practice the last crucial element of sales success – **ACTION**. A plan is not going to just fly off and take care of itself; it needs you to implement it. No one will make those calls for you. Go back to your action plan and write an action step you will take each day to move toward one of your sales goals. If your sales goal is to set three appointments for tomorrow, your action step will be to spend an hour on the phone this afternoon —- today! If your goal is to increase your call-to-closing ratio, your mini-goal may be to finish reading this book. Whatever your goal, begin action immediately.

Notice that once you begin, your energy will increase dramatically.

Throwing the Rabbit

For the next five weeks, make yourself unique by implementing a different success principle each week: Believe—Focus—Knowledge—Plan—Action.

Selling Is a Process, Not An Event

Here are six steps that will take you through the sales process:

- o Make Calls
- o Ask Questions
- o Listen
- o Present
- o Ask for the Business
- o Follow-Up

The order of the sales process is not always the same. You may skip some steps with some clients and repeat some with others.

Chapter 6

Three Great Rules of Selling

After 30 years of hands-on experience, I can share with you my **Three Great Rules of Selling**. This knowledge comes with 40 years of research —- 40 years of reading books —- 40 years of listening to other speakers —- 40 years to discover the three great rules of selling. If you remember these three rules, and practice them faithfully, you will be a success in selling.

Rule #1 in selling: *Make calls.* Rule #2: *Make more calls.* And Rule #3: *Make many more calls.* Are you thinking the rules are too simple; they should be more complicated? Are you saying, "I know that already." Sometimes you need to simply get back to the basics to improve your present performance. It goes back to the IKTA disease, you know, I-K-T-A, I Know That Already. You may know that already, but **are you doing it?** Check your calendar now and review it. How many sales appointments do you have on your calendar this week? Scheduled appointments! Not many? Look at last week. Not many there, right? What about next week? Oh, not many there either, huh?

In 1990, my daughter Ann was my marketing director, and after thirty days on the job, she questioned my three great rules of selling: make calls, make more calls, make many more calls. She had made 300 phone contacts, not counting the 1,300 dials, but had not closed a single sale. She wanted Rule #4. I told her that if I had to formulate Rule #4, it would be to make many, many more calls. I suggested that she continue making calls and report back in a week.

It was one week later that she happily reported her first sale. When I questioned the sale, she realized it came from the contacts she made in the first week of calls. Her second sale came from the calls made in the second week, and so it continued. Her consistent approach to telemarketing created a busy booking schedule for me, 150 engagements one year! Eventually, she rarely made cold calls because she built many strong business relationships over the years, resulting in warm contacts ready to commit.

Taking It To The Next Level

Now take making calls to the next level. While it is important to make calls, make more calls, make many more calls, you can add more power to the system by making targeted, focused, skillful calls.

Targeted Calls

Targeted calls are calls that are made in an industry that fits your profile and your services. Since I was in the advertising agency business, I had experience with media as a buyer and as a media sales person. When I went into the consultant, speaking, and training business, I immediately targeted clients who were in that niche. I was working in a familiar area with persons I knew. Decide what your niche is, and begin there.

Focused Calls

It was natural then to focus on my message because I was on familiar ground. I knew the requirements to succeed from both the seller and buyer perspectives.

Skillful Calls

Becoming skilled at selling is a lifetime project. Becoming more skillful at making calls is a process and not a one-time event. Always be on a quest to improve your sales skills. Develop your professionalism from books, recordings, live seminars, phone seminars, e-learning, one-on-one training, and self-evaluation after each sales call. The most effective training is the training you do for yourself; make it a habit to spend at least fifteen minutes each day improving your craft. Read a chapter from a good sales book, listen to a good audio sales pro-gram, or read a sales magazine.

Take A Clue From Ralph

To prove my point that making calls is vital to sales success, have you ever received a phone call from a computer? How do you respond? Do you hang up? Do you think companies would invest money in those calling machines if they were not suc-cessful? They work! You know why? They play the numbers. I have a client who bought a computer dialer, and I was certain that it would not work. He had the last laugh when he showed me the numbers: 850 dials equal 400 no answers or voice mails, 400 hang-ups, 50 people actually talked to the computer, 15 show interest, and 5 buy. Not bad for a computer.

Here is an example. Make believe I am Ralph the Computer, and I am phoning you. "Hello, this is Ralph the Computer, and I would like to tell you about our wonderful newspaper." (You hang up) Immediately, what does Ralph do? He gets on the phone again and makes another call. "Hello, this is Ralph the Computer, and I would like to tell you about our wonderful newspaper." (Another hang up) What does Ralph do now? Ralph is a computer; he is on the phone again, and Ralph continues to call until someone speaks with him. Eventually, someone will buy.

Now, consider what Joe the sales person does. "Hello, this is Joe with The Daily Bee, and I would like to tell you about our ...OK... you already advertise on the radio. Thank you very much." (—click — hang up) "That sure did hurt my ego. OK now, I think that I will have some coffee to get me back on track." I return to the phone after a ten-minute coffee break, pick up the receiver, and dial my second call of the day. "Hello, this is Joe, and I am with The Daily Bee and I would like to speak with you about...Oh, I see you already —-click—- (hang up) "Oh, that was awful! That person made me feel really bad." So I tell my co-workers, Jim and Beverly. And I tell Greg, and I tell Jane. You see, if I am feeling rejected, I want to take the whole office to my level, to be depressed with me. I do not want to be alone in my rejection. I also call home to my wife to relate how difficult my day is going and how down and depressed I am. Finally I pick up the 200-pound phone to make another call – call #3! "Hello, this is Joe. I am with The Daily Bee, and you are probably not interested in advertising, are you? I did not think so. Thank you very much. Good-bye." —- click —- (hang up) "Whew, glad that call is over."

What happened there? Well, we are humans, not machines. If we let ourselves get rejected or distracted, we make few calls. I guarantee that if you continue to dial consistently, keeping a positive tone in your voice, you could get through just like

Ralph did. Somebody would eventually say, "Hey, I need to advertise. Tell me more." The numbers work.

> **The more sales calls you make, the more opportunities you have to sell.**

Let me relate a true story of a client friend who owns a large dairy in Louisiana. He had trouble with his route sales people, who delivered milk and dairy products door to door. They complained that there was no additional business to sell, but my owner friend believed they were not asking the customers to buy. At the Saturday morning sales meeting, a new man appeared. The owner opened the meeting with, "Hey, how did it go this week, guys?" One of the route men complained again about the difficulty of getting new business. No one was buying. The boss motioned to the new guy Jim to stand up and relate what he did yesterday. Jim said that he knocked on 200 doors and sold 150 quarts of chocolate milk. The route men were stunned when the dairy owner asked Jim what kind of work he did before he came to the dairy, and Jim said he was a garbage man. You see, one day the dairy owner was driving behind a garbage truck when an idea occurred to him. He approached one of the garbage men with a proposition to work a week for his dairy. After working on Jim's appearance, Jim was given a dairy uniform and told to go door-to-door, hold up a quart of chocolate milk and say simply, "chocolate milk." Jim knocked on 200 doors in one day and sold 150 quarts of chocolate milk. All he said was "Chocolate milk." What if he had added, "Delicious, fortified, chocolate milk"? The numbers did it for him. It does not take exceptional skills to be successful in selling. It takes knocking on doors, making many calls. The more sales calls you make, the more opportunities you have to sell. It does not take a genius to do the math, and imagine the results if you combined exceptional sales skills with repeated sales calls! You would be unstoppable.

Just Ten Dials A Day

I had a sales engagement for Lexmark, a company that specializes in high-quality office printers. During my presentation, I gave the 30 participants an action assignment to list ten new business prospects that they wished to meet with. They were instructed to make ten dials, whether the prospects were in or not. In 30 minutes, the participants had made 60 appointments. One participant was elated to get an appointment with a client she had been trying to see for two years. Consider that if 30 people could get 60 appointments by making 10 dials each for 30 minutes, how many appointments could one person get if he made 10 dials a day for 30 days? 60! It is that easy. One person — 10 dials a day for 30 minutes in 30 days equals 60 appointments.

I did the same experiment with over 50 companies and experienced the same results. Each company averaged two appointments per person in 30 minutes. It is important to note the word <u>averaged</u>. Some received two, some received four, and some, none. Over 30 days, you will experience the same success and failure rate; however, in 30 days, you will have 60 appointments or contacts.

Double Your Sales

Now we should discuss the odds in the selling and closing process. On a piece of paper, draw ten circles. Assume that with whatever system you are using to sell now, you are closing 2 out of 10 sales. Darken or color 2 of the 10 circles, representing 20% of the sales closed. When you have completed this book and applied the sales recommendations – key word here –**applied** –you will close 4 out of 10 sales. So color or darken 2 more circles. You will have doubled your sales. Your percentages will vary somewhat from the percentages used here, but I use these circles to make a point. Actually, doubling your sales is not the message that I wish to share with you just now. I will say something a bit controversial, something you do not want to hear. Look at the six remaining unmarked circles. No matter how good your sales skills, no matter how much clients like you, no matter how much you enjoy your work, no matter how hard you try, you are not going to sell everyone. No matter how many sales books you read, no matter how many sales courses you attend, you are not going to sell everyone. Realize that you will lose more than you win in sales, but **do not give up**!

Know that reality if you are going to be a successful sales person. Know in advance that you will find rejection; just persist in the face of obstacles. If you lose a sale, you have five more to lose before you win one. With this viewpoint, you are winning while you are losing. Why waste words: *do not quit* because you face rejection or because your ego has been deflated. *Keep trying*, and you will begin closing 4 out of 10 sales, instead of 2 out of 10. Every month, you have 100 or more windows of opportunity to sell. If you divide every day into one-hour appointments with 30 minutes of drive time in between, you can set 5 appointments in a 9 to 5 day, resulting in 25 appointments a week, totaling 100 or more appointments a month.

If you use a Franklin Planner, Priority Management, or any efficient calendar system, this scheduling idea can apply to those systems. Pencil in or highlight the appointment times for a month on your business calendar. Use the phone to set appointments or fill in the blanks. If you see 100 people per month, do you think you might increase your sales? If you make just three more appointments per day, do you think you might increase your income? Penciling the times in advance is important because every time you glance at your calendar, you know whether you are being productive. If the appointment slots are empty, your sales will be down. What happens when you have extra time because an appointment ended early or was canceled? Try the **triangle approach**. When you exit the building of your previous appointment, look to your left and look to your right. You will see other businesses that can use your product or services. Whether it is down the street or in the same office building, walk in, introduce yourself, and let them know you are in the neighborhood and called on their neighbor.

At this point, your enthusiasm is high, and you want to try some of my recommended sales ideas, so you make a call, and your customer says no. You do not let the rejection get you down, and you try one more time. You try several times, and it does not work. By the time you get six rejections, you begin to think that Joe is a poor sales trainer. You revert to your own tried and true sales approach, and back to closing 2 out of 10 sales, not realizing that you were on the verge of making your first sale with the new approach. Keep trying; keep going. For my system to work, you must use it every time you make a call. That is *every* time you make a call. And believe me, this system works. Begin applying what you learned and begin earning more money immediately.

Leave Your Security Blanket In The Car

The question most sales people ask me is, *"How do I get the prospect to see me?"* I follow many sales persons on appointments, and I have noticed that most feel lost without a briefcase or a stack of spec sheets. On the initial visit, I recommend that they go in "unarmed," without a security blanket of materials, but they clutch tighter to their briefcases and plead to keep them. How does the prospect perceive the briefcase? It is the obvious clue that you are a sales person when he sees you "hugging your security blanket" as you walk through the door, and he is ready to press the eject button. He has only twenty seconds to figure how to get rid of you before you begin your sales pitch. But what would the prospect think if you walk in unarmed, smiling, and alert? Might he think you are a customer? And, how are customers greeted? With a smile and an invitation to enter!

Begin a conversation with the receptionist, speaking with her person-to-person, not sales pest to gatekeeper. Many sales people have difficulty in *finding subjects to talk about with the client.* Become an observant student of your environment. Is there a psychology degree hanging on the wall; do you see any awards; are there clues of special interests like fly fishing, football, or art? Base your questions on your sincere curiosity and add a sense of humor to your comments. Be observant and look for areas that others would miss. Certainly, other sales people have crossed that bridge before, and most comment on the family photographs in the office. Set yourself apart, do not look for the obvious, but find unique topics for conversation.

> **Base your questions on your sincere curiosity and add a sense of humor to your comments.**

Over the years, I have learned a more natural sales opening. As an example, I mention the time that I entered a prospect's office and noticed a harpoon hanging on the wall. Now, this was no ordinary harpoon; Captain Ahab could have used this one to conquer Moby Dick! So I casually commented, "I must ask a question. You really take your fishing seriously, don't you?" We laughed, and the client relaxed and opened up to me. We talked about him, his home in New England, fishing, whales, and how he loves to collect marine memorabilia.

> **You always have something to talk about if you use your radar to find it.**

I cite another time that I called on a prospect and asked how long he had been flying. He was curious how I knew he was a pilot. I pointed to the wall, where a framed Jeppesen pilot map was displayed, and commented, "Not many people would hang one of those in the office, would they?"

Another question: *How do you get past the receptionist on*

a cold call? I can answer this question with another example. Once, when making a cold call, I entered the business and found myself standing between two desks and a secretary sitting behind each desk. I smiled and asked, "OK, which one of you has the most influence with Frank?" One secretary pointed to the other and said, "She does." So, I addressed my next question to her, "Are you as good as she says you are?" She leaped from her desk and said, "I will be right back." Dragging Frank by the hand, she returned to us in the reception area. Could I have used a script here? No way. Look for the opportunities, and the most important thing that I stress here, do not take yourself so seriously. Be natural, and have fun.

Throwing the Rabbit

Successful sales people are the ones who **do** the things that unsuccessful sales people do not do. Make calls; make more calls; make many more calls—and you will be Throwing the Rabbit over the heads of your competition.

Chapter 7

Ask, And You Shall Find Out

When making sales calls, you need the skills to be effective. The most important component in selling is the ability to ask questions. Many years ago, I was in a sales training program conducted by Fred Herman, salesman extraordinaire and author of *Selling Is Simple.* Fred told us of the time he was on a TV show, and the host, knowing of his legendary salesmanship, challenged Fred to sell an ashtray. Now, place yourself in Fred's shoes and imagine that you are on national television, and the announcer puts you on the spot, hands you an ashtray, and says, "Sell me this ashtray." What would you do? What would be your approach? Fred Herman paused a moment and asked, "Well, what would you do with the ashtray if I sold it to you?" The host answered, "I do not smoke myself, but people are always getting ashes on my furniture and on the floor, so I guess I would use the ashtray to keep the place neat." Fred looked at him and said, "And, what would you pay for an ashtray like this?" The host replied, "I would say about $5." Fred smiled and said, "Sold! You have bought yourself an ashtray for $5!" Fred made the sale by asking just two simple questions.

The most important component in selling is the ability to ask questions.

The power of what Fred did is lost in its simplicity. The average sales person, in the same situation, would have picked up the ashtray and said something like this, "You mean this beautiful white ashtray? Look at the pretty design in the center, and notice that it holds six cigarettes instead of just four, as a normal ashtray does, blah, blah, blah.... It is made right here in the good old USA too, blah, blah, blah.... And look how sturdy it is, blah, blah, blah, blah...." And when the salesman completed his sales pitch, the buyer would say, "Well, I do not smoke." Where do you go from there? The genius of Fred's approach is that he used simply two questions to make the sale.

I will take you through the process to skillfully ask the effective questions. The questioning approach will increase your sales and build stronger relationships with your customers. Using effective questions positions you differently than the sales person down the street because it shows you care about your customer. When asking questions, if you *focus on finding the best way to serve your customer*, you will intuitively ask the right questions.

In a previous chapter, I mentioned positioning yourself as a serve person. Many customers perceive selling as something the sales person is doing TO them. When you consider yourself a **serve person**, you do something FOR and WITH your customers. Your attitude changes, and you sell more as a serve person because you approach the sales process with the customer's interest in mind, not your own interest. The customer is better served, and the relationship continues beyond a one-time sale.

There are **three sells to every sale**. First you sell yourself, second you sell your company, and then you sell your product. If the customer does not buy you, he will not buy the company or the product. And how do you sell yourself? You sell yourself by asking questions and by showing an interest in your customer. The truth is that people like you because of the way you make them feel about themselves. From this time forward, think of yourself as a serve person, always interested in the needs of the client. I may use the word sales person for simplicity; however, continue to think of yourself as a serve person.

> **People like you because of the way you make them feel about themselves.**

One of my clients, taking me literally to change his image, reprinted the business cards for all his representatives, using the new title Serve Person, instead of Sales Representative. The first time the new business card was presented to a client, the client said, "What is this Serve Person?" When the sales person replied, "Well, I am not here to sell you; I am here to serve your needs," the client smiled and said, "Well, it is about time!"

When you have the serve person mentality, you focus on the client, not on your wallet. You focus on the client's needs and on how you can help him. When you accomplish that, you become a professional serve person without realizing it. So, if you want to be a great sales person with a servant's heart, ask many questions to know what the customer's needs are in order to propose a solution. That tells customers that you are there to serve them, not to sell them. Remember this, *telling is not selling.*

> **Selling is getting inside the customer's head by asking questions, and the only way to know what the customer is thinking is to ask instead of to tell.**

I will give you an anchor, or word picture, to remind you to ask questions instead of smothering your customers with unwanted information. The word picture, something you can live by on every sales call is: stop vomiting on your customers! I know it sounds crude, but I guarantee that you will not forget it the next time you are face-to-face with a customer. I have observed that one of the biggest problems in selling is the over-zealous sales person who throws up on his customers. Picture this —- an eager sales person, with catalogs and graphs in hand, makes a great first impression when he greets the customer warmly. They sit down, and the sales person figuratively begins to throw up with too much information, "Our product has been around for 25 years; we are the best in the business; and here are some of the graphs to demonstrate my points." He vomits needless information, and meanwhile, the prospect develops a glassy-eyed look, and his attention drifts.

Stop vomiting on your customers!

Until he asks questions, the sales person is clueless as to what the customer wants. He can assume that it is quality the customer wants, but all he really wants is price. Or he can assume that price is significant, when the truth is, quality is the major decision factor. It is impossible to create value for the customer until you have discovered the hot buttons. Until you know what makes them happy, telling is not selling. Telling is a self-centered sales technique that is ineffective, compared to the art of asking questions. Ask yourself, has any client kicked you out of his office while talking about himself? Probably not. If you talk about yourself and your wonderful product, you will never have the relationship with your client that kindles repeat business.

> **Telling is a self-centered sales technique that is ineffective, compared to the art of asking questions.**

As part of my research for training, I accompany reps on sales calls to observe their techniques. One example was Jane, a rep from a print supply company, who entered a reception area in the standard opening, "Is John in?" The receptionist stated that John was out, but Bill was taking his calls. Jane replied that she had been calling on John for two years, so she would return another time to see him. I suggested that since we were there anyway, why not see Bill. When Bill agreed to see us, Jane pulled out a thick catalog of 40,000 printer parts and accessories and began, "Well, we appreciate this opportunity to be here. Let me, if I can, show you a few of the things we can do for you." As she flipped through the catalog, I noticed that poor Bill was glassy-eyed. I have this theory that if a person does not blink every seven seconds, his attention is naught, and he is in La-La Land. When I realized he was not blinking, I knew we had a problem, and worse still, I looked over at Jane, and she was not blinking. Real problem! Both were in a daze. When I interrupted to ask Bill some questions, I noticed Bill's relief that he would not have to endure the entire catalog presentation. The conversation went something like this:

Joe: Do you buy much printing supplies, Bill?

Bill: I sure do.

Joe: Who else, other than you, gets involved when you make a decision to buy?

Bill: Well, nobody. I make all the decisions myself.

That was two years down the tubes for Jane because she had been calling on the wrong person. It is so easy to simply ask, and of course, ask diplomatically. If you asked outright who the decision-maker is, you appeal to ego, not the truth. Ask the question, "Other than you, who else gets involved in making this decision?" This technique makes it easier for the customer to answer honestly. If there is another decision-maker, immediately get that person in the room, or ask what would need to exist to get him/her involved in the conversation. Asking questions is important, but if you address the wrong person, you waste your time and their time.

> **"Other than you, who else gets involved in making this decision?"**

To finish the story, I continued to ask questions about him and his business, and the prospect went on for thirty minutes. In the process, I discovered that he was using printing plates from the competition. So I asked, "Ever have any problem with those plates?" He said, "No, never." I countered, "Never?" He replied, "Never." I repeated, "Never?" He faltered, "Well, yes, come to think of it, I have had a problem." (Prospects tend to answer more truthfully when the question is asked three times.) I questioned, "What was the problem?" He answered, "Well, sometimes their plates do not hold water." Now, I know that toning results when plates do not hold water, and the presses must be stopped, and five people stand around with nothing to do. Five unproductive employees mean lost sales and late deliveries, so it is Joe to the rescue because I know all his problems, and I have the solutions. Is it time to vomit sales information and solutions? I could explain how my products can solve his problems, but when I finished, his eyes would be glazed over again.

> **Prospects tend to answer more truthfully when the question is asked three times.**

Ask questions that cause him to feel his pain:

Joe: And what happens when you have plates that do not hold water?

Bill: You get toning.

Joe: And what happens when you get toning?

Bill: I have to shut down the presses.

Joe: What happens when you shut down the presses? How many people do you have standing around twiddling their thumbs?

Bill: I have five people standing around with nothing to do.

Joe: Are they still on the payroll?

Bill: Yes, they are.

Joe: Is it possible, just possible, that you might lose a client because of this?

Bill: That almost happened.

Joe: Tell me about it.

People buy for one of two reasons – pain or gain.

Ouch!

When you discover where the bruise is, let him relate his painful experience and relive it all over again. Bill told me that a client gave him a job at 9 pm and needed it by the next morning at 6 am. Bill assured him that he could meet the deadline, and normally he could; however, at one in the morning, there was a toning problem. The presses were stopped for a while, and it was tight meeting the early morning deadline. It was close!

Joe: You made the deadline?

Bill: Just barely.

Joe: Sounds like you were not happy with that situation.

Bill: I hated it.

Joe: Are you familiar with our plates?

Bill: Sure.

Joe: Have you had a demonstration of our plates?

Bill: No.

Joe: May we give you a demonstration?

Bill: Sure, if the plates can hold water and do what
you are telling me.

We presented a product demonstration, and now Bill buys
all his plates from Jane. That is how simple it is to ask questions versus telling.

How do you decide which questions to ask? Here are five
suggestions that will empower you to be a better serve person—
to stop throwing up on your customers—to arm you with the
information to fully benefit from the next phase of my selling
system:

➤ While reading the daily newspaper, look for articles about
your customers that will stimulate new ideas and new
ways that you can serve them better.

➤ Read industry publications. If you work with printers,
read their association newsletters. If you work with
bankers, subscribe to the American Bankers Association
magazine. Look for trends in their business and for ways
that your company can play a part in those trends.

➤ Form a customer council, made up of your key customers,
and hold a monthly meeting or call them individually to
discuss current challenges. You may get business just for
including them on your council and for showing an interest in their business.

➤ Call your customers periodically to remind them that you
are available to help them. Many of my clients have been
delighted with my spontaneous calls that came just when
they were searching for a speaker for their next meeting.

➤ Write notes often. Write your customers on birthdays,

before special meetings, when you see an industry article about their company, and write them even when they reject your proposal. Be top-of-mind when the time comes, and they have a need for your product or service.

Develop The Right Questions

A sales person should not wing-it when approaching a prospect, and scripted approaches are less effective. If I gave you a list of questions to ask prospects, you would sound canned and insincere. My questions would not relate to what you need to know about your client. Recently at a convention, another speaker heard me tell my audience to never use a script. We spoke later, and he admitted that he disagreed with me, that he taught sales scripting. He cited the movies, where actors use scripts and sound very natural. I paused a moment and thought about his observations. I asked, "Have you ever seen a bad actor?" He answered, "Sure." I replied, "I rest my case."

> **A sales person should not wing-it when approaching a prospect.**

Sales people are not trained to be professional actors. Although I can teach people to sell in three days, I cannot teach them to be actors in three days. Even though I do not favor scripting, I do believe in preparation by working backwards in the sales process.

Look at that process now by writing ten reasons why I should do business with you, the sales person. This will take a little time and thought. *If you fail to find ten good, solid rea-*

sons for doing business with your company, how is the customer going to find reasons to do business with your company?

State each reason in one or two words. For example:

Results

Service

Delivery

In Stock

Quality

Selection

Value

Versatility

Location

Me (the sales person)

Make a list of your reasons why I should take money out of my pocket and put it into your pocket. You may wish to record your reasons on a 3x5 card and take them with you on a sales call to prompt yourself. Remember this card is not a license to spew information on your customer, but rather, an opportunity to turn each reason into a question or series of questions. Try this: As you glance at the first reason **results**, you might ask the question, "How do you measure results when you invest in widgets?" Or you might state it another way, "What is the most important results you desire when purchasing widgets?" Or, "Results, how do you determine the results you are paying for?" Notice that it does not sound scripted because you are phrasing the question as you look at the reason list. Spontaneously base your question on the key word results, and you will sound natural and sincere. Now, come up with three questions based on results to entice the customer to purchase your product. This is a good practice exercise.

How do you know what to ask next? Go to the next reason on the list, right? No. You are still working on results; ask as many questions about results before moving on to the next reason on the list.

> **You get the questions to ask about results by listening to the customer's response to your question(s).**

Good listening is the key. If you ask what the most important results you desire when purchasing widgets, the customer might answer that he wants widgets to fit his specifications. Instead of glancing at your card and asking a question about the next item on your list *service*, ask him another question based on his response. Inquire about those specifications that he mentioned. Example:

Customer: I want widgets that fit my specs.

Sales person: What specifications are important to you?

Customer: Well, the size and shape are very important to me.

Sales person: That sounds interesting, and what shape will please you and your customers?

Customer: Round.

Sales person: Why round? Why is round important to you?

Customer: Because round fits more of my customers' applications.

Sales person: I see. Now, what about size? What is the

best size? We talked about shape, now what about size?

Continue until you have exhausted the subject, and then move on to the next subject. Try this as a segue into the next line of questioning:

Sales person: We have talked about results, and you said the shape and size are the two most impor tant factors, (now you glance at your 3x5 card and see that **service** is the next topic) what is your definition of good service from a widget supplier? Since people have differ ent definitions of service, what is your defi nition?

Customer: Prompt response.

Sales person: Sounds as if you may have had a situation where you didn't get the response you were expecting. Is that true?

Customer: Yes, I have had a situation like that.

Sales person (Here goes the pain button again!) Really? Tell me about it.

Continue with this line of questioning until you have cov ered all ten reasons on your card. The process will prevent you from vomiting reasons on your customers, and at the same time, it will aid in discovering whether your product or service really suits their needs.

The power of asking questions has helped me out of tough situations on many occasions. I can remember the time when I finally landed an appointment with Ron, the chairman of a national trade organization, from which I sought a speaking engagement. I flew to New York for the sales call, where Ron hurriedly escorted me to his office, telling me that he promised me thirty minutes, but could give only five. He prompted me to give him ten ways that I could help his organization.

Did I know ten ways to help his organization? Sure I did. I knew them off the top of my head, but I knew better than to throw up all over Ron. As tempting as it was at that moment to give Ron the information he requested, I questioned Ron instead, "What ten things do you want to see happening at your upcoming convention or your next meeting?" He rattled off ten things, and I nodded my head and said, "Good. Now Ron, listen, I can do nine of the ten. How important is that tenth one?" The following scenario ensued:

Ron: Well, to be honest with you, the tenth is not critical. You can do the other nine?

Joe: I sure can.

Ron: Then, you have the job.

I accomplished the sale with two questions. After I left Ron, I contemplated the rhetoric that I would have vomited without asking a single question. Ninety percent of my presentation was off target! It was not that I could not accomplish the ten things that he wanted, but that I just did not know what the ten things were. You must know the client's needs before you can help him. So take the time to turn your reasons into questions, so that if your reason does not appeal to your client, you can move on to the next question. You can assume you know what a client wants, but until you ask, it is only a guess. You must ask to discover the real need.

> **You can assume you know what a client wants, but until you ask, it is only a guess.**

I am teaching concepts that you can apply to the real world. If I give you a set script, you would forget it in a week and return to old, familiar ways to sell like everyone else. But if I teach you a concept, you will adapt it to your own unique style. You will begin to sell **three-dimensionally.**

Do you remember when you learned to drive a car? From the time you were born until you were sixteen years old, you watched your mom and dad drive. Although you were ready, you had to take driving lessons. Remember that initially it was uncomfortable, and you held both hands on the wheel, white knuckles, and it was difficult to stay in your lane. But today, do you still get in the car and say, "Put the key in the ignition, put the car in gear, and drive forward?" Of course not, you drive by instinct.

The same thing will happen to you with this questioning technique. Initially, you will be uncomfortable and feel that your questions are prying. I assure participants in my sales seminars that in the real world, asking sincere questions is not a problem with clients. Ask as many questions as you wish because you are no longer a sales rep; you are a consultant to your clients. Does a doctor feel that he is prying? Would a doctor diagnose your problem without questioning your symptoms? How long have you had fever? Have you been vomiting or coughing? After getting your responses, the doctor could prescribe a treatment. You felt better about him because he questioned until he could diagnose your problem.

The doctor example is analogous to selling. If you are customer-focused on client problems and needs, very rarely will the client call your meeting to an end. Speak in terms of the client's interests by asking questions and being attentive to the responses, and you will have earned the right to discuss your product.

> **Speak in terms of the client's interests by asking questions and being attentive to the responses.**

So what about your product? How important is product knowledge? Many companies spend weeks training in product knowledge, but neglect sales skills. What happens then? The company has a huge force of sales people who vomit product information on their customers because they know too much. If they knew a little less and focused on the art of consultation, the customer would be better served. I know this works because I did some field work with a client who sells Microtox Laminate equipment. Although I am not familiar with the product, when I worked in the field with their sales people, I sold more product than they did because I was customer-focused instead of product-focused. I asked the clients about the most important thing about the equipment, and they were happy to answer. Although I understood little about their responses, I asked the natural segue question, "Why is that important to you?" When the client asked a technical question, I deferred the answer to the sales person accompanying me. **The goal is to learn the**

client's needs, not to spew off how wonderfully made the product or service is. Product knowledge will serve you better in the later presentation phase, because if you know how to ask questions, you can design solutions that will solve their problems.

What Does It Sound Like In The Real World?

We have covered the basic principles of asking questions, and now some practical applications with role plays of situations you might encounter in the real world. They demonstrate ways to use questions in the sales process.

Imagine that I am a newspaper sales person, speaking with a potential advertiser, Mason's Department Store. We are past the introductions, and I begin to ask questions related to getting results from the newspaper. Whether newspaper advertising or widgets, substitute *your* product and apply the concept to your product or service because this is a new way to ask questions using your very own style and personality in a very natural way.

Remember that you begin with the first word on your list, and in this case, the first word on *my* list happens to be *results*. You develop a question in your mind by looking at the key word *results*. (Notice that I said in your mind, not on paper). You do not move on to the next question until you have exhausted the first question, getting valuable information from the potential client. Here is the scenario:

Joe: Ann, I noticed your advertising on radio and television. What segment of the audience is your customer?

Ann: Well, I am trying to reach the younger market

Joe: Ah, I see, the younger market. Is that the market that is important to you?

Ann: Well, yes, many teens shop here.

Joe: Teens, huh. Is this something new, or have you been in that market for a long time?

Ann: Well, actually, no, this is a new venture for us.

Joe: New venture. So you are reaching out for a completely new audience, and why is that?

Ann: We feel that they are the ones with the big bucks now. They have credit cards.

Joe: They do have the credit cards, and do many of them have a Mason's Credit Card?

Ann: Some, but not enough.

Joe: So you are advertising to get them to visit your stores and to get a card at the same time?

Ann: You might say that.

Joe: What kind of results are you expecting?

Ann: The more cards we get out there, the better.

Joe: How do you measure those results, if the customers do visit?

Ann: Well, we can track the credit card volume to see if they are responding to what we are doing.

Joe: So, currently the only way you measure is volume, in other words if the people are coming in, the volume increases, is that true?

Ann: Yes.

Joe: Would it help if you had something tangible that

would show you exactly where customers found the idea to visit your store?

Ann: Well, of course.

Joe: And, it sounds dumb to ask this, but how would that help you?

Ann: We would be better able to stay on top of our sales.

This is where most sales people jump in and attempt a trial-close.

> **Although the client may give you signs of interest, never trial close. NEVER trial close.**

A few years ago, I was conducting a seminar before an audience of 300 people. Several in the audience worked for a large corporation whose sales training is based on the trial close. Since they were drilled on the trial close, when I stated to never trial close, they nodded their heads in disbelief, and I noted their reactions. I said, "We can vote to see which is the better approach. You are the buyer, and we have a good dialogue going, but every time you give me good buying signals, I jump in and try to close. Will you want to answer any more of my questions?" Several responded that they would feel manipulated or would lose trust in the sales person. It was a unanimous decision that trial closing is manipulative.

> **If you truly have a serve person's mentality, you will be more interested in gathering the information you need to serve the prospect's needs.**

It is not time to close the sale because you are still in the process of developing a rapport. You do not trial close when selling three-dimensionally because in the big picture of the sales process, the relationship is more important than the process. Keep first things first, and everything else will fall into place to close when the time is right.

Here is what a trial close would look like at this point in our presentation:

Joe: Well, how would knowing the results help you?

Ann: We would be better able to stay on top of our sales.

(Now here is the trial close):

Joe: So if you ran a coupon promotion in the paper, one that had an application form, you could better track whether or not your advertising is working, could you not?

(The buyer sees where you are going, and becomes more cautious in her answers.)

Ann: Well, I am not really sure.

(That is not the answer you were seeking, so pick up where we left off before we tried a trial close. We will continue to seek information by asking questions.)

Joe: How would knowing the results help you?

Ann: We would be better able to stay on top of our sales.

Joe: And how would that help you?

Ann: Well, invest our advertising dollars more wisely.

Joe: And then what would happen?

Ann: I guess we would increase our sales.

Joe: Would that affect your ad budget?

Ann: Yes, we could increase it.

Joe: How could it benefit you personally if you could increase your ad budget?

Ann: I could show my boss how the advertising is working!

Hear the difference? Talk in terms of her interests. Remember what she says so that you can use it later in the presentation phase of the sales process. And you are not presenting until you have gathered more information. Notice I have not asked questions about anything but *results* so far. I asked questions based on her answers. I listened to her responses, sometimes repeating them, and then I designed the next question based on what she said. After gathering all the information about *results*, I can move on to the next item.

> **Listen to the responses, sometimes repeating them, and then design the next question based on what was said.**

(But first take a look at what would happen if your approach were an inflexible script. Let's role play that one.)

Joe: Hi, I understand you are advertising on television and radio, is that correct?

Ann: Yes.

Joe: *(OK, next question, service.)* What kind of service are you getting?

Ann: Great.

Joe: *(OK, budget.)* What is your budget?

Ann: I do not know you; that is none of your business.

OK, what do you ask her now? Your clients do not have the same script that you have. Sometimes they say things that are not in your script, so if you really want to ask powerful questions, listen to the answer, and develop your questions based on the answer. Then it becomes a natural dialogue, a conversation. Have you ever taken a call from one of the major banks selling credit cards? The call goes something like this:

> Hello, this is First Bank. May I speak to Mr. Bonura, please? Hello, Mr. Bonura. How are you?
> I am fine, you are fine, we are all fine!

When selling over the phone, never ask the customer how he is doing. You do not know the person, so why should they believe you care? It is also the signal phrase that implies I am a telemarketer, hang up on me. Telemarketers obviously use scripts; they should vary their introductions every so often.

Nido Qubein, a fellow professional speaker, tells how he outwitted one of those callers. He received a call, and the telemarketer asked him if he would mind answering a few questions. He said, "Sure, but first, can I ask a few questions?" The caller began to stutter because that was not on the rehearsed script. Then Nido asked, "Where are you calling from?" "Huh?" "Are you married?" "Uh, uh, yes." "How many children do you have?" "Uh, uh," *click.* The caller hung up because he was flustered that Nido was not following the telemarketer's script. You will never experience this when using my questioning technique because you are in control of the entire presentation. Look at the information that I discovered from the Mason's Department Store prospect; I discovered that she was already using radio and television and that she was not advertising in the newspaper. I encouraged her to talk about her advertising and about why she advertised with the competition. It is good information to understand why she is happy with her present situation. In the end, she was happy with them because they had a way to measure results, and I knew that our way of measuring results was better. There was no other way I could have known what she really wanted without asking the questions. I will use the information later when I give the actual presentation.

Suppose you feel **Reputation** is a reason for doing business with a company. We can role play using that one word. Remember, the word is just a reminder, a catalyst to get the gears going in your mind, and you make up the questions to provide a stimulus for the client's responses.

Joe: You know, Ann, to most people, reputation is important when they do business with a company. How important is it to you?

Ann: Very important.

Joe: How come? *(Now, notice I use the words "how come." It is not Grammatically correct, but it sounds softer than "why.")*

Ann: Because I need to trust the sales person, who will be handling my money.

Joe: And how come trusting someone, who deals with your money, is so important?

Ann: Well, because without trust I could be out of business.

Joe: That would be awful, would it not?

Ann: Yes. *(laughing)*

Joe: Have you worked with someone with a bad reputation?

Ann: Yes! And we lost big!

(Now here is the pain button. Listen to the next question.)

Joe: Would you tell me about it?

Ann: When he invested my money in shaky dealings, I lost all of it.

Joe: And how did that make you feel?

Ann: Cheated!

Joe: Have you heard of our firm?

Ann: Yes, from my friend Joan, who said you made her investments grow.

Joe: From what you already know, would you say we have a good reputation?

Ann: Yes.

Do you see where this natural form of questioning leads? If you had a script, you would be so focused on the next thing to say that you would not be focused on the client's response. With this method, you can listen comfortably and develop your questions based on what you hear from your client. With this method, you must listen to formulate the next question. It is a **customer-focused approach**.

What happens if the prospect has no interest in a reason you thought would be important to him/her. Observe the following role play:

Joe: Is price important to you?

Ann: No.

Joe: What makes you say that?

Ann: I am more concerned with quality. Since you get what you pay for with a widget, I want it to work and last a long time. I believe that if I paid less, I would get a widget that lasts only six months, and then I have wasted my money.

Think about this scenario. What have I learned? If I had assumed that she was concerned with price, I might have turned her off when I promoted our great, low price in my presentation phase, so now I know to emphasize quality, not price.

What if a reason to do business is **location**? How can I turn location in our favor?

Ann: You are too far away.

Joe: Well, actually many people tell me location is the most important thing to them. However, how important is proximity when you have a problem, and the sales person down the street cannot solve it because he does not have a service attitude or the expertise?

Ann: I guess if he cannot solve it, his location is irrelevant.

Joe: So how would it benefit you to do business with someone who may be farther away, but he would give you the service you want?

Ann: Well, I guess I would get the results I want.

Who said it? She did! Not me. Now look at it from another

angle: What if she lives close by? Observe the role play:

Joe: How important is the convenience of working with a company only blocks away?

Ann: Well, I deal with a company across town, and they give me good service.

Joe: So when you need service, you want it, right?

Ann: Yes! And I want it immediately.

Joe: What situations might arise in your business that would require immediate service?

Ann: When my equipment is down, delivery to my clients is a problem, and it makes them angry.

Joe: Sounds like it could cost you some business?

Ann: It sure could.

Joe: Okay, let me ask you something else...

I can change the subject here because I have enough information to move to the next question. I will keep this information for later in the process when I present the reasons for doing business with me.

During one of my sales seminars in New York a few years ago, I was role playing when a man in the back of the room blurted out that my questioning method would not work in the real world. The dialogue went as follows:

Joe: Oh? Sorry. How come you feel that way?

Man: Because it is so obvious when you start asking people questions like that.

Joe: Well, what is it that is obvious?

Man: People know when they are being manipulated, and they will not play along with you when you ask questions.

Joe: Is there something I said that makes it so obvious that they would not respond to the questions? *(The class began to catch on at this point. I was asking questions, and he did not feel manipulated because he was focused on our natural dialogue.)*

Man: Sure, people are not so dumb that they do not realize that you are asking them questions; it is obvious.

Joe: What can't they realize?

The class began to laugh, and he finally caught on, and conceded that the questions could work. When there is a real dialogue, the other person is not thinking that he is being manipulated because if you are honest and sincere and interested in serving, your prospect will not feel intimidated.

> **When there is a real dialogue, the other person is not thinking that he is being manipulated.**

Besides finding out the needs and desires of your prospect, you will discover the critical things like who is the decision maker, and what is the decision-making process. Here are some examples of how to go about it without bruising egos.

Joe: Is there anyone, other than you, who gets involved in making the decision?

Ann: Yes, Carla.

Joe: Carla?

Ann: Carla Jones. She is the VP of marketing. She holds the purse strings.

Now at this point if I was thinking about closing the sale, and I have never spoken to Carla, I have a problem. Unless Ann is a super sales person and totally passionate about my product, she is incapable of selling my product to Carla. Here is the next step:

Joe: I have not met Carla. Have you told her about our product?

Ann: No, not yet. She is very busy.

Joe: Then, let me ask you this. If Carla did not have the decision to make, what would your decision be?

Ann: Oh, I am very excited about the product.

Joe: Wonderful! Just what is it about our product that you like?

Ann: I like product quality and your service.

Joe: What is it about the quality that you like?

Ann: The product will make us look good to our clients.

Joe: And, what about the service?

Ann: Well, as I mentioned before, that is the biggest problem we have had lately, and you demonstrated how on-target your service is. I especially like the testimonial from ABC Corporation.

Joe: All right, so is that what you will relay to Carla?

Ann: Yes!

(Now is the opportunity for me to meet Carla.)

Joe: You know, if you feel that strongly about my product, I can help you to present it to Carla. Does that make sense?

Ann: It does, but she is hard to reach.

Joe: Maybe we could try right now. Do you know her extension?

One of two things could happen now. She is either going to arrange a meeting, or she will insist on relaying the information to Carla.

Ann: Yes, I know her extension.

Joe: Well, see if she can meet with us on Friday at three o'clock.

If this approach works, I have an opportunity to sell the decision-maker; however, she may wish to handle it on her own. If that happens, at least I have confirmed what she feels about the product and what she will say to Carla. She likes the product quality and the service. Sometimes we simply speak with the person who will influence the decision-maker, and yet, not have the opportunity to speak with the decision-maker. Of course, always remember **the fastest way to the sale is through the main decision-maker.** Now to return to the dialogue:

Joe: Then suppose we set a time to meet with you and Carla to discuss the possibilities? Does Friday look good?

Ann: Great to me.

Now I have the opportunity to sell the decision-maker and still include the person who will influence the decision-maker, but know that the fastest way to a sale is through the main decision-maker.

Throwing the Rabbit

Let people know that you care about them more than you care about yourself by being genuinely interested in what they have to say. In other words, speak in terms of the client's interests by asking questions and being attentive to the responses.

Chapter 8

Come Out, Come Out of Your Comfort Zone

Most people have trouble asking questions because they have small comfort zones. You usually have a small area of comfort that represents the way you react to life. There are areas beyond your comfort zone that represent a potential or growth in your life. It could involve singing, public speaking, selling, fears of any kind. Each of these activities and your response to them varies by individual. Today public speaking is within my comfort zone, but it was not always the case. It may be well beyond your comfort zone; however, you may put bungee jumping in your comfort zone, but that would be out of my comfort zone! We usually do what is most comfortable for us, but we could be flying airplanes instead of simply driving delivery trucks because we do not go beyond the comfort zone.

Coming out of your selling comfort zone can be very painful, so to avoid it, you do not make the sales calls. You live under the illusion that if you avoid the sales calls, you eliminate the pain. Although you will not experience pain immediately, you will feel it when you cannot pay the bills because you do not have the income. If you know that you will experience pain anyway, why not experience it immediately and make some money at the same time.

So how does it work in the real world? In my class seminars, I select someone to sing the national anthem, and most of the time, I get an emphatic refusal. Once I was surprised when I asked an audience member to sing, and she leaped to her feet and passionately sang the anthem from beginning to end as if she were a professional. The audience gave her a standing ovation! I asked her how she could perform so well, and she told me she was an opera singer. It was a coincidence that I chose the one person who could perform the task that most people would never attempt. She was the wrong person to demonstrate my point about comfort zone! For some people, singing in public is in their zone, but maybe flying an airplane is not. Each of us has unique fears.

Besides skill, the situation could determine your comfort zone. What if I asked the same woman to sing the anthem before 60,000 football fans at the Super Bowl? Under those new conditions, she might have a different response. Most people live in their comfort zones for their entire lives.

> **You will succeed in life in direct proportion to your willingness to come out of your comfort zone.**

You can change your comfort zone by facing your fears, and learning a new skill that will eliminate your fear. I have. When I was in high school, my greatest fear was public speaking. I remember studying for a test to name the fifty states, and the teacher asked me to recite them in front of the class. I was prepared and knew the states, but when I stood before the class, I lost my voice. I could not remember the states; I was petrified.

Later in life, I realized that if I did not overcome my fear of public speaking, I could never reach my potential. I enrolled in a public speaking course. Instead of ignoring my fear, I faced it and forced myself out of my comfort zone. Today I speak to thousands of people every year in my speaking career. In fact, today I speak so much that my wife bought me a tee shirt that says, "Help! I'm speaking and I can't shut up!"

So what can happen if you stretch a little? Try coming out of your comfort zone, step-by-step. Ask one more question than you normally would. The second time ask two tough questions. Here is a role play to see how you can grow one level at a time, beginning with Level One:

> **Joe:** My name is Joe, and I am with First Bank. I would like to speak with you about your banking needs.
>
> **Woman:** I bank with National Bank.
>
> **Joe:** Oh...oh...Take my card, and if you ever have a problem with your bank, you will call me, right?
>
> **Woman:** Sure.

OK, what happened there? I gave her my business card, I ran out of the bank. What do you think happened to the business card as soon as I left her? She tossed it, right? Now, go to Level Two:

> **Joe:** My name is Joe, and I am with First Bank. I would like to speak with you about your banking needs.
>
> **Woman:** I already bank with National Bank.
>
> **Joe:** Great, because we like to speak with people who understand the value of a good banking relationship.

May I have a few minutes of your time?

Woman: I am happy where I bank.

Joe: Thank you very much. Here is my card.

Now that was better, but go a little further out of your comfort zone. Move to Level Three:

Joe: My name is Joe, and I am with First Bank. I would like to ask you some questions about your banking needs.

Woman: I already bank with National Bank.

Joe: Great, we like to speak with people who do business with good banks. May I have a few minutes of your time?

Woman: I am happy where I bank.

Joe: Well, I can appreciate that you are happy with your present bank. Are you familiar with Conner Furniture?

Woman: Yes.

Joe: Rite Choice Pharmacy?

Woman: Yes, I am.

Joe: Mike's Moving Service?

Woman: Sure.

Joe: All those companies felt the same way you do, and now they are very valued clients of our bank. Do you have about fifteen minutes?

Woman: Actually, no, I am busy now.

Joe: Well, OK, thank you very much. Here is my card.

We move closer to the prospect by asking some key questions to arouse their attention. We were zooming out of our comfort zone to the point where it was very uncomfortable, right? One more time: see how far we can go with Level Four:

Joe: My name is Joe, and I am with First Bank. I would like to ask you some questions about your banking needs.

Woman: I already bank with National Bank.

Joe: Great, because we like to speak with people who understand the value of doing business with a good bank. May I have a few minutes of your time?

Woman: I am happy with my bank.

Joe: I can appreciate that you are happy with your bank. Are you familiar with Conner Furniture?

Woman: Sure.

Joe: How about Rite Choice Pharmacy?

Woman: Yes.

Joe: Mike's Moving Service?

Woman: Yes.

Joe: Well, all those companies felt the same way the first time I visited with them, and today they are very valued customers of our bank. Do you have about fifteen minutes?

Woman: No, I am busy now.

Joe: I can understand that now is not a good time. I have my calendar here, and I see you have yours on your desk. Can we set a more convenient time for you?

Woman: Well, all right, Monday at 4 would work for me.

Joe: I will jot it down here on my calendar if you will do the same.

Woman: Done.

Now, why do I go to Level 4? The average customer has two turndowns, and the average sales person has only one comeback. I figure that if I keep asking, eventually the prospect is going to see that I am serious. Do not let fear take over because your ego has been bruised. That is why movie theaters are open during the day: A place where wounded sales people can hide when they should be out selling.

> **Do not let fear take over because your ego has been bruised.**

One of my clients, Robert Havrilla, shared a story with me that a sales rep had been calling on him for five years without getting any business. Finally the sales rep gave his card to the receptionist and said in a friendly voice, "Please tell Mr. Havrilla that I have not seen him yet, but I will call on him until I do." The receptionist gave the card to Robert, who was so impressed with his persistence that he caught him in the parking lot and gave him a chance to meet with him. The rep got the business because he had the courage to keep trying.

You will be nervous too when you are trying new things, but with practice, fear wears off. At one point in my career, I was frightened of flying! I did not want to go near an airport, but it was necessary because my clients were all over the country. So what did that mean? I had to white-knuckle every flight; I practically pulled the handles off the seat. I knew I could not continue living that way because by the time that I arrived at my meetings, I was wiped out emotionally.

I painfully remember an episode driving ten hours to Oshkosh, Wisconsin, from Louisville, Kentucky, to avoid flying. My client asked why I drove instead of flying, and I made a lame excuse that photography was my hobby, and I liked to take pictures along the way.

I knew I was making excuses for staying in my comfort zone, so I was determined to do something about it, and I signed up for flying lessons. My first thirty hours was in a plane with an instructor, and after that, I was ready to fly solo. I remember my solo day as if it were yesterday. My instructor exited the plane commenting, "Well, no need in killing both of us!" That sure gave me confidence! Nervously, I taxied to the end of the runway, then I pushed the throttle forward, and the plane rushed ahead. As I pulled on the yoke, the plane lifted and I was airborne. Yahoo! On my first solo, I was required to do three touch-and-go's (we like to call them crashes-and-dashes). You must touch the wheels to the ground, lift off, circle around, repeat the cycle three times. By the time I completed the requirements, I felt very confident. I had completely conquered my fear of flying, and I was enjoying the experience. I now travel by air over 100 days a year.

Do the thing you fear to do, and the death of fear is certain. Learn the skills required for your trade. Learn how to sell, and you no longer fear it. When you do something that you fear, it places you on the edge. And when you are on the edge, what happens? The adrenaline flows, and you get more meaning out of life, and enjoy it at the same time.

Do the thing you fear to do, and the death of fear is certain.

I have also come out of my comfort zone as a buyer, which is uncomfortable for me because when I want something, I just want to buy it without a hassle. This time I wanted to purchase a set of drums, a full set of drums! I had to come out of my comfort zone to negotiate with the sales clerk. When he mentioned the cost, I told him that I had budgeted much less for the set, but throw in the cymbals and it is a deal. To those remarks, I got silence. But I knew the strategy to his silence: first one to open his mouth, loses. So, even though I really wanted those drums, I too was silent. He waited, then walked over to the cymbals and replied, "I will give you the cymbals, but not the seat." I knew the cymbals were about $80, so I asked, "How much is the seat?" He said, "$40." I said, "I'll buy the seat, you give me the cymbals, but throw in a pair of drumsticks." Now the drumsticks were only about $5. By stretching myself out of the comfort zone, I received the cymbals, as well as the drumsticks, as part of my deal.

Be conscious of your present comfort zone, and stretch it every chance you get. Decide to ask one more question in the sales process, or give a presentation in front of a large group of people. Keep stretching, and before you realize it, you will have expanded your possibilities.

Try this exercise to expand your comfort zone. Write all the things you enjoy and feel comfortable doing. These represent your comfort zone activities. Then record all the things you feel only moderately comfortable doing and would like to do. These represent a moderate step out of your comfort zone. Now write the activities you would like to do but feel *very, very* uncomfortable doing. (Do not include bungee jumping if you have no desire to jump and would not feel a sense of accomplishment from it). Record activities that would make you a better person, but you have feared them. For example, if you have always wanted to submit your stories to <u>Readers' Digest</u>, but you were afraid to do so, write that possibility. Having those stories published would boost your self-confidence and encourage you to write. Stretching yourself to submit your stories would be a positive comfort zone objective.

Make an effort this year to perform two possibilities that stretch your comfort zone. Make an appointment with yourself to check this outcome next year. Only you have the ability to expand your comfort zone. Next year, do this exercise again, including additional ways you can expand your possibilities. You will find that as time passes, you will conquer more and more of your fears, and your objectives will get bigger and bolder.

Throwing the Rabbit

You will not succeed in selling if you have your head hidden in the sand of your comfort zone. Throw the Rabbit by taking your head out of the sand and going places in the sales process where you have never been.

Chapter 9

The Ears Have It

Hopefully, you can see the importance of asking questions. Look beyond the process of asking questions and realize the invisible part of the sales process. What should you be doing the entire time you are asking those questions? **Listening**, of course—the key to practicing three-dimensional selling.

> **Anything you propose to the client later, will be based on what you hear.**

Problem-solvers listen and turn challenges into solutions. The only way to design creative solutions is to listen intently to the client's needs and desires. When audiences hear my questioning skills in classes, they mistakenly think that I have a question-asking skill, but really, I have a listening skill. My next question is based on what the prospect says when answering my previous question.

Do, what I call, **bounce-back questioning**. For example, someone says, "I like baseball." I would respond, "Baseball? What do you like about baseball?" Or, if a client commented, "Customer service is rotten at most companies," I would ask, "Rotten? How come you feel that way?" Simply reflect on the client's response, and in this way, the client feels understood. You are assuring the client that you have heard and understood what was said. It is a natural response, and the customer does not suspect a hidden agenda.

This concept came in handy on a vacation trip to Germany. Carol and I have been married for 40 years, and I like her to think that there are still things to know about me. Prior to the trip, I bought a set of tapes on how to speak German. Actually they were called, *Getting By In German*. Without Carol's knowledge, I listened to the tapes daily during my drive times. By the time we left for our trip, I knew enough German to get by, and to play a prank on Carol. When we arrived at the airport in Germany, I hailed the cab using my new lingual skills, *"Taxi bitte."* Seeing that the cab responded to my command, Carol looked at me suspiciously, but she did not comment at the time.

When we dined out that evening, I called the waiter to our table, *"Herr Ober? Herr Ober?"* and he came to our table. Excited about my new skill, I said, *"Zwei Tassen Kaffee, bitte. Mit Sahne. Kaffee Coffein frei."* I had ordered two cups of coffee with cream and specified decaffeinated coffee. Carol was surprised, but she continued to say nothing of my impressive language skills.

After dinner we went to a store, and the sales clerk did not put our purchase in a bag. So, I thought, "Oh great! Something else from my German tapes." I knew how to say bag. I looked at the woman and said, *"Eine Tüte bitte."* The woman reached behind the counter and handed my wife a bag. Carol could not hold back any longer. She said to me, "OK, tell me what is going on." I said, "I have been listening very closely, and the language is very easy to understand and learn. Listen closely, and you will pick it up quickly." She shrugged her shoulders in disbelief and remained quiet.

The next day we took a train trip, and while we were sitting in the train's passenger compartment, a German woman passed by, and I called to her, *"Komm nehmen sie platz bitte,"* which translates "come in and have a seat." So the German lady entered our compartment and sat down. Assuming that I spoke German, she spoke German to me, but I had no idea what she was saying, and I certainly did not want Carol to know. So, using an active listening technique (bounce-back listening), I repeated her last word in a questioning tone. I mixed a few oohs and aahs and hmms. At first I could understand some of what she was saying, but then she began speaking too fast to follow. Occasionally, I said, *"entschuldigung,"* which is "excuse me," and then looked over to Carol to tell her what she was saying, fabricating everything. The woman nodded her acceptance, "yah, yah," truly believing that I was translating the conversation. This procedure continued for quite a long time when I began to worry that the woman would begin to ask questions instead of making statements. Knowing that it would soon become obvious to all that I was not in control of the situation, I excused myself and remained in the dining car for the rest of the trip. I returned just in time to wave goodbye, and say, *"Auf Wiedersehen!"* She waved back, *"Auf Wiedersehen!"* Carol looked at me and said, "You amaze me." She said that with such sincerity that I finally confessed my scam, and of course, she was suspicious of me for the rest of the trip.

This story certainly demonstrates how important active listening can be. Our little German lady knew nothing about me because she wanted to talk about herself. If you use positive body language, verbal signals, and bounce-back listening, your clients will tell you everything you want and need to know in order to key into the sale. The biggest problem most sales people have is listening because they are focused on their next question or statement, and they do not pay attention to the answers. With bounce-back listening, you must listen attentively because your next question will be based on how the client responds.

To prove my point further, a role play situation would be helpful. Suppose that I am a newspaper sales person selling advertising to a home improvement store:

Joe: Could I ask you a question? You invest in advertising, right?

Woman: Yes.

Joe: How come?

Woman: To bring customers into my store.

Joe: I see. And how is it working?

Woman: Pretty good. It could be better.

Joe: What do you mean when you say it could be better?

Woman: Well, if I had more customers I would certainly make more money.

Joe: And what would you consider enough customers to put a smile on your face?

Woman: About 10% more customers than I had last week.

Joe: Ten percent more than last week? What did you do last week to bring in the additional customers?

Woman: I ran an ad in your competitor's paper.

Joe: Oh, and how did it work?

Woman: Not so good. We did not see any additional business. I guess I should try something else, huh?

Joe: How come?

Can you see what I did? When she said she should try something else, I did not say, "Great, I am the something else! You have the right person right here!" What did I say? I said, "Why would you do that?" I threw her off base. Return to the dialogue in progress:

Joe: Why would you do that?

Woman: I have new products and new people moving into the area all the time.

Joe: And, if you were to make a decision to do something else, what would be the most important thing to you in making that decision?

Woman: Well, if that decision could bring new people to my hardware store, new faces, new people who would spend more money."

Joe: Is that what is really important to you: people spending more money? Can I see a copy of that ad you ran last week?

Woman: Sure.

Joe: Who did the layout and the concept?

Woman: A college student.

Joe: Oh, I see. So, maybe it was not the media that did not work. Is that possible?

Woman: Yes.

Joe: Could it be possible that the creative or the message did not work?

Woman: Yes, I suppose so.

Joe: May I ask a question? *(I reach into my pocket and take out a $20 bill and a $1 bill)* If you had a choice, which one of these bills would you want?

Woman: (laughing) The twenty dollar bill

Joe: But why, look at the two bills. Would you agree that they are both printed on the same size paper, or media?

Woman: Yes

Joe: Would you say they both have the same color ink?

Woman: Yes

Joe: Would you say that overall, they look alike?

Woman: Well, yes

Joe: Then why would you pick the twenty?

Woman: (laughing) Twenty dollars is better than one.

Joe: So, if the media is the paper, is it the media or the message? You see, do you want a twenty-dollar message in your ad or do you want a one-dollar message in your ad? Why not let us put an ad together for you? We will see if we can come up with a $20 idea. Does that make sense?

Woman: Yes.

Joe: How come it makes sense?

Woman: (laughing) I guess because you are the expert.

Joe: You know how to sell your product, and I know how to help you sell it, right? So let us help you put an ad together, OK?

Woman: Great.

Did we make a sale there? The sale was that I earned the right to put an ad together for the client. We actually closed on the intention of the call. Did you notice that all my questions were formed from the responses of the client? Visualizing little branches of a tree, picture little branches of questions growing out of the client's comments. The more branches you see, the more active listening you are practicing.

I have two exercises for you to try. First, practice bounce-back listening with your family, your friends, or your associates. Listen closely to their responses and reflect their words with questions. You will be amazed how people open up and share their feelings and thoughts when they see that you are sincerely listening.

Try another listening exercise at home or at your office. Do not reveal what you are doing and see what happens. *(Now, I do not recommend experimenting with this one on your clients.)* When someone speaks with you, do not make eye contact, but look away, look at the floor, or look at the ceiling. Do not look them in the eye. What happens? You observe that they stop talking or get tired and irritated with you. See what a difference it makes to use your whole body in the listening process? Just averting your eyes makes a huge difference.

Let me share **the eleven traits of a good listener**:

❖ A good listener looks at the speaker and uses **Eye Contact**.

❖ A good listener does not finish the other person's sentences. There is nothing more irritating than trying to express an original thought when someone cuts in and assumes the rest of the statement.

❖ A good listener uses **positive body language**. Keep your arms open, and not crossed, to indicate that you understand their ideas. Occasionally, nod your head or shrug your shoulders to get your body involved in the process of listening.

❖ A good listener uses **positive verbal signals**. Say, "uh-huh," or "hmmm," or "I understand." As the speaker gives you information, these verbal signals, which give positive feedback, will reveal that you are in the conversation. Imagine the confusion if you telephoned someone, but they made no response when they answered the phone. You would continue to ask, "Are you there?"

❖ A good listener uses **positive facial expressions**. Smile often, even when on the telephone; it shows up in your voice. Let concern show on your face when the speaker expresses a problem.

❖ A good listener does not change the subject too quickly. Let the speaker express concerns and ideas fully before you move on to a new subject. Concentrate on finding out their needs; do not interject your own stories and experiences.

❖ A good listener asks questions to prompt further discussion. As I mentioned earlier, develop your questions from their responses, and you must be attentive to accomplish that.

❖ A good listener focuses on what the speaker is saying,

and not on his/her own next statement.

❖ A good listener exhibits patience. Do not look at your watch or tap your fingers on the table or look over the shoulder of the speaker.

❖ A good listener uses the 80-20 rule. Simply stated, you speak 20% of the time and you listen 80% of the time.

❖ A good listener **makes the speaker feel important**. Imagine that the speaker is wearing a sign that reads, "Make me feel important."

Commit these eleven points to practice and always remember that **in the sales process, the only time we learn is when our ears are open, and our mouths are closed.**

Throwing the Rabbit

A rabbit's foot may bring you luck, but rabbit ears will get you the business. So open your ears, and you will open the customer's heart.

WHO WANTS TO BE A SUCCESS?

ANSWER THESE

* WHAT IS THE PRODUCT OR SERVICE?
* HOW DOES THE PRODUCT SERVE OR WORK?
* WHAT DO I GAIN OR NOT LOSE BY
  PURCHASING YOUR PRODUCT OR SERVICE?
* CAN YOU PROVE THAT EVERYTHING
  YOU HAVE SAID IS TRUE?

Chapter 10

Give Them What They Want

The next step in the sales process is presenting. There is a time for everything, and finally, this is your time to speak. After asking questions and listening, you have earned the right to present. If you have nurtured your client to this point, he/she will be willing to listen. Consider what the client needs to know before making a decision to do business with you. You might ask that question directly to the client, if you have not already.

Here are a few standard questions you should be prepared to answer before the sale is made. The following are **what clients want to know**, whether they have verbalized the questions or not:

- ❑ What is your product or service?
- ❑ How does your product or service work?
- ❑ What do I gain, or not lose, by purchasing your product or service?
- ❑ Can you prove that everything you said is true?

Write the questions on a 3x5-index card or business card and put them in your wallet, purse, or briefcase. Review and answer each question before you make any sales presentation. The following is a role play, incorporating the questions in a sales contact with a client:

Joe: How do you pay your monthly bills?

Woman: I use my First State checking account.

Joe: I see. And what made you decide to open a checking account with First State?

Woman: Well, when I moved to town, my neighbor recommended the bank.

Joe: Oh, have you been pleased with their service?

Woman: Very pleased.

Joe: What is it about the checking account that pleased you most?

Woman: It is convenient because I do not have to carry cash everywhere I go.

Joe: I see. And what else do you like about the checking account?

Woman: I do not have to pay for the checks.

Joe: Great. Anything else?

Woman: No, not really.

Assume that you are in the presentation phase of the sales call; it is your turn to speak. This is how you convert the information you gathered in the questioning phase to a presentation. First, ***What is your product or service?***

It is a checking account that is a convenient way to pay bills. Now, the next question: ***How does your product or service work?***

It offers many conveniences such as safety, tax record keeping, and budgeting. And then, ***What do I gain, or not lose, by purchasing your product or service?***

We can answer that in a role play:

Joe: You mentioned earlier that you liked your First State checking account because your checks are free. Is that correct?

Woman: Yes.

Joe: Other than that feature, is there anything else that makes you happy about your First State checking account?

Woman: I cannot think of anything else.

Joe: Now if you could have your checks free and also have no service fee on your checking account, would you be interested in knowing more about it?

Woman: Sure.

Joe: What appeals to you about that arrangement?

Woman: I could save in two ways: one way on the checks and another on the monthly service fee.

Joe: Correct. And all you have to do is maintain a $1,000 balance in your checking account. And you mentioned earlier that you usually do have a balance of about that much, is that right?

Woman: Yes.

Joe: Then, what would have to exist for you to begin saving money by opening a checking account today?

Woman: Well those things sound good, but I am comfortable with my present bank.

Now, here is where you utilize that last question: ***Can you prove that everything you said is true?***

Look for the answer in this role play:

Joe: I understand that you and Mary Smith are good friends.

Woman: Yes, we went through school together.

Joe: Did you realize that she has been a customer of our bank for over ten years, and she loves her checking account. What if we would just pick up the phone and give Mary a call right now?

Woman: Not necessary; if it is good enough for her, I guess it would be good enough for me.

Joe: Sounds like you are ready to open an account now.

Woman: I am ready.

Joe: Good, then you can start saving some money too.

For further proof, have with you testimonial letters from happy clients or a reference list with phone numbers. Ask the client to call one of the numbers if it will help in making a decision. Say something like, "Sometimes people do not take testimonial letters at face value, so I told Mary that I would be visiting with you today, and she gave me permission to call her. Can we do that now?" That gives powerful credibility to your case.

To make a persuasive presentation, create a vivid picture in your prospect's mind, helping him visualize all the benefits of doing business with you. If you listen carefully to what the client says in the questioning phase, this part of the sales process will come together very easily. Convert the "wants and needs" into convincing word pictures.

For example, when selling advertising space for a newspaper, and the number of subscribers is important to my client, I might say, "Have you seen Freedom Hall, the sports stadium in Louisville, Kentucky? It holds over 20,000 people. Well, our newspaper has a circulation of 400,000. Now, imagine yourself sitting in the center of Freedom Hall, and the stadium is full of your customers. You have a chance to show every one of them your product. Then that group leaves, and you can show your product to 19 more groups of the same size. Do you think that would have some impact on your business? What if you could do that every week?

The secret is that you are not selling circulation, or even numbers. You are selling bodies! Forget numbers and sell the picture because it creates a stronger impact. Do not simply say, "Hey, you can reach just as many people as it takes to fill Freedom Hall 20 times." No! Get them to envision themselves in the middle of that stadium and to see masses of people surrounding them.

Try some exercises to sharpen your presentation skills. Choose a prospect whom you have already interviewed to research his or her needs. At the top of a sheet of paper, write the prospect's name. Then write the product or service that would benefit that person. Then answer the question, what is it? How does it work? What is the gain to the prospect? Can you prove what you said is true? Notice that the benefits can change according to the prospect's needs or desires. While one may benefit from your quality and fast delivery, another prospect may benefit from your price or your toll free service number.

Call on your designated prospect and use the information

you recorded to give a presentation. Continue to practice this process each time you make a sales call. You may not have the answers to all four criteria until you have met with the prospect. You already know what your product is and what it does. You can pre-plan proof in most cases, but do not assume the benefits to the prospect. Your best bet is to ask the prospect.

As I mentioned earlier, there are only two reasons people buy from you. One is pain, and the other is gain. If they **do not buy** the product, they will experience **pain**. If they **do buy** the product, they will experience **gain**. As human beings, we want to avoid pain and experience gain.

While I was conducting a seminar, a woman commented, "Oh, Joe, that is not true." I told her, "Of course it is. Everything you have bought was motivated by pain or gain. Mention any item you bought over the weekend, and I will prove my statement." She said, "OK, deodorant." She gave me an easy one. "Great! Why did you buy it?" "Well, I like to put it under my arms after a shower." "How come?" "Because it makes me smell good." Now there is the *gain button*. "Why do you want to smell good?" "Because I do not want to offend people." "Why do you not want to offend people?" (Getting closer now!) "Because they will not like me." "And that would be painful, would it not?" "Yes, it would. OK, you win." Did I make my point? You want to avoid pain and to experience gain. Your job is to find the prospect's pain and to get them to re-experience the pain, and then you can give pleasurable solutions. You can recreate the pain during your questioning phase. Here is an example of how to do that:

Joe: Have you ever had poor customer service?

Woman: Oh yes, just last week.

Joe: Sounds like it really bothered you. Tell me what happened.

Woman: Well, I called the Closet Carousel to come to my home to give me an estimate to organize my closets.

Joe: And what happened?

Woman: I had budgeted a thousand dollars for the project. I set an appointment for Saturday morning at 9 o'clock. Now, I do not usually get up early on Saturday morning, and maybe I should have made the appointment later, but I woke up early on the one day of the week that I am able to sleep late. Well, 9:15 am rolled around, and the closet man did not show. Ten o'clock rolled around, and still he did not show, not even a call.

Joe: How did that make you feel?

Woman: I was fuming. Maybe I should have realized that this might happen because when I made the appointment through the manager, I could hear the rep in the background grumbling about possibly going hunting on Saturday.

Now you have a working idea of poor service as seen through your client's eyes. Dependability is important. Clarify that point by asking, "I take it dependability is important to you then?" Unless you have completed your questioning process and know everything you ever wanted to know about the prospect, do not mention your dependability yet. Here is what most sales people do during the questioning phase:

Joe: Have you ever had a bad customer service experience?

Woman: Yes.

Joe: Well you will not find bad service at our company.
All our reps are great. You see, we are very, very, very
good at service. One thing client's love about us is
our service…blah…blah…blah.

See the difference? In the second example, I did not find
what the specific problem was with service. The client must
relive the experience, feel the pain, and share the story. Your
concern and willingness to listen will make a difference. Wait
until the presentation phase to make your point about the bad
experience and to give proof that it would not happen with your
company. Try this in the presentation phase:

Joe: Remember when you told me about that awful experience you had with the closet man? You said that
reliability is important to you. At our company, we
have systems that prevent no-shows from happening.
Our receptionist will call you the day before to confirm the appointment, then she calls the sales associ-
ate to reconfirm with him. We have never had a problem with no-shows. Does that sound like a workable
plan?

So use the pain to make your point. Turn their pain into a

gain for your company by showing how your product or service will ease their pain. It also demonstrates to the prospect that you were listening. That is the difference between a problem solver and an order taker.

Throwing the Rabbit

You will be Throwing the Rabbit with your presentation skills when you answer the following questions for your potential clients: who, what, when, where, why, and how.

Chapter 11

Ask, And You Shall Receive

The next step in the sales process is **asking for the business**, or gaining a commitment. Some call it "closing," but that term is not productive because closing implies an ending. For a true consultant, selling is an on-going process; it does not stop at the close because a true serve person will develop a relationship that will continue.

> **You do not close sales—you open relationships.**

Do you realize that you are already a born sales person? Everyone is. I can prove it with a story about my granddaughters. When my daughter-in-law gave birth to twin girls, those four-pound baby girls were the best sales persons I have ever seen. At one day old, they got anything they wanted. How did they get it? They cried because it was the only way they could respond. They asked for the business. Somewhere between the time you were born and the time you received your business cards, you lost the ability to ask for the business. If you executed every step of the sales process perfectly but never asked for the business, you would seldom make a sale.

> **Somewhere between the time you were born and the time you received your business cards, you lost the ability to ask for the business.**

Have you ever pushed a five-year-old through a checkout counter in the supermarket? If you have not, you have certainly observed someone who did. Why do you think they put the candy at the checkout counter? "Daddy, can I have some candy?" "No, you cannot have candy." "Daddy, please can I have some candy?" "I said, no, you cannot have candy." (Now listen to the next question she asks.) "Daddy, how come?" (Now, this child has never taken my sales training course, and listen to the brilliance of her last question) "Daddy, how come I cannot have any candy?" (She is finding out the objection. You cannot sell until you know what the objection is, right?) So Daddy gives her the objection, "Because you will not eat your dinner." (Now she handles the objection.) "If I promise to save the candy until after dinner, can I have it?" "I said no!" "Please?" "OK, here, take the candy." What do you want to bet that she eats the candy on the way home before dinner? She will plead, "I promise I will eat my dinner." "I said no!" "I Promise." "Just eat the candy, and please do not tell Mommy."

Why do we lose that persistence? At five, there is no fear, but somewhere along the way, we learned a fear of rejection. Why are you afraid to ask your clients good, solid questions that could lead to the sale? The first sale was to get the candy in her hand, and the second sale was to eat it on the way home. Ask yourself what is the worst thing that can happen if you ask for a commitment? They might say no. What do you get if you do not ask? Nothing. So, if the result is nothing anyway, why not try?

If there is something to gain by trying, and there is really nothing to lose, just ask.

Now I could teach you a course on 35 ways to close a sale. You know them: the either/or close, the Ben Franklin close, the puppy dog close, the right uppercut close. The list goes on and on, but you do not need 35 ways to close a sale. Besides, customers are too sophisticated these days because they have read all the books on closing that you have. If your customer feels manipulated by some sales line, you have damaged his trust.

You need only one way to get the business: Two words – write this down – two powerful words – JUST ASK! That makes it easy because there are no tricks, no silly games, no techniques, or manipulations. If you make the sales call, ask the questions, listen to the answers, and present a creative solution, then all that remains is to ask for the business. There is no one perfect way to ask, but simply ask. If you are selling advertising, try, "Can we put you in this week's edition?" Or, "Can we put you on the air this week?" If you are selling insurance, use, "Would you like to have this policy?" If selling consulting services, you might ask, "Can we have a commitment for September 24?" It is not brain surgery—It is simple—Just ask for the business.

Throwing the Rabbit

"It ain't what you say; it is how you say it," especially when you are saying what the customer wants to hear. Throw the Rabbit by feeding back to the customer his/her own words.

Chapter 12

The Sale Is In the Follow-up

The last step in the sales process is **follow-up**. Sadly, this is where more sales are lost than any other time. The average sale is made after the fifth call, yet the average sales person follows-up only once or twice. The sales process can take one call in some cases, especially when dealing with a quick decision-maker. The process may take five calls or five years.

> **As long as you have a qualified prospect, be persistent.**

Here are some tips for follow-up:

✓ Have something worthwhile to say on your return visit.

✓ Write a thank you note for the visit as soon as you get to your car. Carry stamps and note cards in your car.

✓ Send the prospect a published article on their industry.

✓ E-mail the prospect with a product fact.

✓ Keep detailed notes of your calls so that you will know where you are in the sales process; it is natural to forget or to confuse one client with another.

✓ Always schedule a follow-up date while you are with the client, or it will not happen.

✓ For appointments, use a paper system, or better yet, a computerized system, which will save you time and make your personal marketing processes easier.

Follow-up with clients is so easy with computer and special software packages. Computers enable you to write a single letter or mail a group of letters with a few keystrokes. You can search your database for clients in a specific industry and schedule appointments instantaneously. Organize your day and take your phone calls from a daily task list. With special software, my computer dials numbers quicker than I could dial them by hand, and there are no misdials. I have customized my contact software so that it includes the questions we ask to qualify a prospect.

A computer is cumbersome on the road, so invest in a small notebook, the 59-cent spiral variety, the kind that fits in your coat pocket or your purse. When you meet a prospect or client, make notes while your ideas are fresh and then transfer them to your computer later.

Know as much as possible about your client. Use your notebook to record the information. Know what the client eats for breakfast, children's names, and college alma mater. When you follow-up later, use the information in your conversation: ask about the horses on his farm, or his wife Sally, or comment on how his university beat its archrival last week. The client will be impressed that you remembered and will be softened further with your follow-up. This is what separates the super sales person from the mediocre sales person. Be sure that you do this out of sincerity, and not out of manipulation.

Throwing the Rabbit

In selling, repetition is the mother of memory. Multiple exposures to the client will make you "top-of-mind" when decision time comes.

Chapter 13

Dial For the Dollars

This special section is devoted to using the telephone to your advantage. You may use the phone to qualify prospects or to make appointments, or you may go through the entire sales process using the telephone. Either way, you will find some ideas here to help you work more efficiently by phone. Prepare a list of prospects and their numbers. If you have a computer, schedule and set reminder alarms to create a call list. Always have more names than you intend to contact, because no matter how many dials you make, you will probably only contact about 30% of the decision-makers.

In our office, we have developed a system to measure telephone sales success, and I highly recommend that you do the same. We track daily, weekly, and monthly dials, and additionally, we track contracts, hot prospects, and sales. If you do not know your track record, it is difficult to set new goals. Our industry research shows that if you make 30 dials a day (30 phone calls), and you have an intermediate sales skill level, you will reach 50 contacts per week, and 8 of those will be hot prospects moving toward a sale. Of those 8 hot prospects, we make 2.5 bookings a week. (Notice I said 2.5—We have this thing to an exact science, to the decimal point.)

As your skills improve, so does your contact rate. Keep a log of your calls, daily and monthly, to determine your call-to-sale ratio. Your numbers may vary from ours, depending on whether your product or service is a high-ticket or quick-sale item. Once you know your numbers, you will know exactly how much activity it takes to produce the desired results.

Make a daily appointment with Alexander Graham Bell. Set aside the same time each day to make your telephone calls. Basically, make an appointment with yourself, note it on your calendar, and then show up. If you only use the phone to make appointments, and not to sell, set aside one or two hours a week for the task. Focus on only one thing during that time: the phone. That means no jumping up to write letters, to mail packages, to make proposals, or to get an extra cup of coffee. If you focus, you can average about ten or more dials every thirty minutes.

Always begin your call session by preparing yourself mentally and physically. Stand up, move around, and get your blood flowing before and during call time. Sit on the edge of your seat, or stand up, and your vocalization will become more powerful and energetic. Use a mirror to check yourself to smile while you speak. It really works! Come out of the dark ages if you still use a hand-held receiver. It is no wonder that you stop calling after fifteen minutes: your elbow and neck can only take so much strain! Here is a life-changing suggestion: switch to a headset. You will use the phone much longer without growing tired. You avoid elbow, back, and neck pain, and you keep your voice alive and friendly. Once you begin dialing, do not stop for anything; the momentum will fend off call reluctance.

Okay, another question you might have is, "What if I get caught in the voice mail jungle?" Well, let me guide you through that jungle. The first rule of voice mail – if you have the option of reaching a live person, take it! Usually dialing zero after the beep will get you to an assistant or a receptionist. Ask for the assistant's name and say, "Linda, I was in Bob's voice mail. What is the best time to reach him in person?" Call back at the suggested time. If you are unable to reach him at that time, forward to the assistant again, and say, "Linda, I was unable to reach Bob at the time you suggested. I wish to leave a message; however, I am tough to reach, and I want him to avoid phone tag. How can I reach him now?" You will be amazed at how often you will find your contact by simply asking the question. This does not work every time, but you will have a better chance, maybe a 30-40% better chance of reaching your prospect.

> **The first rule of voice mail – if you have the option of reaching a live person, take it!**

In our technological age, we encounter voice mail so much that it is surprising when we reach real live people. Be ready to convert your voice mail script into a human conversation. I can appreciate that voice mail can be a disheartening obstacle for sales people who are cold calling for prospects. **A cold call** is one where you reach a person who does not know you, was not a referral, or was not expecting your call. So, if you get voice mail on your initial dial to a cold prospect, give only your name and your company. Since it is your responsibility to reach the prospect, do not give your phone number because you will frustrate your prospect, especially if you are difficult to reach. If you leave your number on voice mail or with a secretary, you have relinquished control of the situation. When you call back, the secretary can say that he has your number and will call you back when he has a chance. Believe me, if it was a cold call, they will never call you back. Instead, try this approach:

"This is Joe from ABC Company calling. Sorry I missed you this time. I will call back this afternoon. Please expect my call." You have raised the prospect's curiosity level, and you may increase your chances of reaching your contact. Another approach to reach Bob is to set a telephone appointment on his voice mail.

> **Setting a telephone appointment reduces phone tag and increases your chances of reaching your prospect.**

Your message might sound something like this:

"This is Joe calling from BTS and we work with organizations that want to increase sales and improve customer service by providing top-notch training programs. I missed you the past few times I called, and well, I do not know you, Bob, and you do not know us. I am not sure we can help you until I know more about your company, so I would like to set a ten-minute telephone appointment to ask you a few questions. Would you please check your calendar for either 4 o'clock tomorrow afternoon or maybe 10 o'clock Wednesday morning? I will be calling your assistant this afternoon to see if we can confirm one of those times. I look forward to speaking with you. Goodbye."

How do you survive in the voice mail jungle when making **warm calls**? Warm calls are calls to people who already know you or who may be familiar with your company. You might want to get in touch with them to confirm or to make an appointment or just to speak with them again. If you are out of the office most of the time, leaving messages with your phone number can aggravate prospects because when they return your call, they may get your voice mail. So what do you do to alleviate getting lost in the voice mail jungle for both you and your customer?

Here are seven **field-tested techniques to use voice mail** to your advantage when making warm calls:

❑ Prepare your points before you make the call. State your purpose clearly, and then ask for what you want them to do. Be specific, and you will save time, stay more focused, and be less likely to leave out anything. Do not write out the exact words because it will sound scripted; just have the main points.

❑ Include a benefit statement, and give them a way to respond. If you expect them to return your call, you must give them a good reason to do so. Remember the pain or gain motivation that we talked about earlier? Design your own personal benefit statement and put it in a question format. For example, "How would you feel about saving $100 on your monthly gas or electric bill? We may be able to show you how to do that." Keep up with their industry, and when you learn something about your prospect, especially in a news story, use it to get their attention. For example, your voice mail script could read, "I heard that you are creating a new telemarketing department. Are you aware that my company offers a seminar series to help telemarketers to overcome the jitters of making cold calls?" Now here is the important part if you want to leave your phone number. Suppose that you were on the other line when the customer returned your call and reached your voice mail. To avoid that situation, your voice mail message should say, "I'll be in my office between 2 and 3 pm today. Please give me a call at 1-800-444-3340. If you get my voice mail, I am on the other line. Just leave your name, and I will return your call as soon as I hang up." You told them in advance what time to call, and you warned them that they might get your voice mail. I used my 800-number for them to call me. Many sales people vacillate on whether to use a toll free number in their messages; however, real-world experiences taught us that customers are more likely to respond if the call is free. If you have a toll-free number, use it.

❑   Use a referral if you have one. For instance, if you were given a lead by Bob Jones, use his name in this way, "I promised Bob Jones that I would give you a call. He hired my company to train his sales people, and he is experiencing phenomenal results. He felt that you might like it too." Notice that I did not say, "Bob Jones gave me your name." His immediate response to that would be, "Why is Bob giving my name to a sales person." A referral is a warm call, so leave your name and number as I suggested.

❑   Always deliver a detailed message when recording. Just

think of it as a one-way conversation that your contact will eventually complete. One advantage to voice mail is that you can ask for exactly what you want and be assured that it is communicated in the way you want to say it. Secretaries and receptionists may misinterpret your message to a prospect. That happened to me recently when I asked the secretary to have her boss call me at 3 pm, and she told him that I would call him at 3 pm. When he did not call, I knew something went wrong so I picked up the phone and called him. Depending on his secretary could have cost me a good opportunity.

❑   When leaving a phone message, you must create a sense of urgency by giving the contact a pressing reason to call back. Give date deadlines, or let the customer know you are low on inventory. For example, "Hi, Bob, this is Joe Bonura. I will be in Chicago on January 19, and I will be conducting a seminar on negotiating long-term contracts. I knew that you would want a reservation, so if you give us a call by next week, we will reserve a spot for you. But call as soon as you can because space is limited. Hope to hear from you soon. Goodbye." Never lie about deadlines or stock to create urgency; it is not worth your reputation.

❑   Create a voice mail script that is interesting or unique. Add your personality, sound effects, singing, music, or anything attention-grabbing. I have a colleague who uses dialects and impressions to get callbacks, but be sure to use discretion. Determine whether your uniqueness is appropriate to the situation based on your familiarity with the contact. Leo Burnett, the advertising great, once said, "If all you want to do is get attention, walk down the street with a skunk on a leash. You will get attention, but it will not be favorable." Our objective is to get a callback, not simply their attention.

❑   Be clear and concise. Keep your message to thirty seconds or less, preferably less. Preparation is the key to keeping your timing sharp. Practice your message several times before making the call.

With a little effort and some patience, you will improve your return call ratio by thirty to forty percent. Get started now on those calls and practice what you learned. If you tried all my suggestions and still you cannot reach Bob, try this option. Fax your prospect a fax-back sheet that has all the questions you need answered to determine whether he is a qualified prospect. Leave space for him to answer the questions and to fax-back a response.

The following are **suggested questions to include on your fax-back sheet**:

➤   Are you the person who makes buying decisions regarding our product or service?
➤   Who else would you involve in that decision?
➤   Are you interested in knowing more about how we can help you?
➤   Are you using a competitive product or service now?

- ➤ If yes, which one?
- ➤ What would you change about your current product or service?
- ➤ Do you need more information about us?
- ➤ What questions do you have for us?
- ➤ Should we continue to call on you?
- ➤ If yes, what is a good time to call?

We tried this fax-back option on a prospect that was extremely difficult to reach by phone, and even though he gave us his business card and asked us for information, he was too busy to speak with us. Realizing his situation, I figured that it might be easier for him to write his answers to our questions rather than spend time talking during working hours. We devised a comprehensive questionnaire that would help us design an action plan for him. We faxed it to him with a request for completion and for a telephone appointment to discuss it. A few days later in the mail, we received the completed questionnaire, including his company's press kit. The successful result was a booking for four days of my sales training. He later confided that he appreciated that we cared enough to learn about his business before making recommendations. He was impressed that we were respectful of his time, and we were pleased with the efficiency of the fax-back system.

Here is another suggestion to contact that hard-to-reach prospect. When a friend of mine had trouble getting a customer to return his calls, he went to the local toy store and bought a large toy phone. He made a label with his telephone number and pasted it on the face of the phone. He mailed the phone with a note that read, "Been waiting to hear from you. Thought I would make it easier for you to reach me." The next day, he received a call from a laughing client. It worked! Be creative, use your imagination.

Okay, so you tried all the phone techniques, and nothing worked. If possible, and if the account is worth the investment of your time, consider actually knocking on his door in person. If you are still unsuccessful, it may be time to move on. Time spent being turned down by a hard-to-reach prospect can sometimes be better spent going after other prospects. Roughly five calls on the same prospect with no response is a sign to pitch the lead. The secret to making successful cold calls and warm calls is a quantitative list of potential prospects. Spend your energy on a new lead, and you are more likely to get favorable results.

Throwing the Rabbit

Set a goal to become a telemaster instead of a telemarketer by daring to be different by using the principles in this chapter.

Chapter 14

Real-World Concepts From a Real-World Sales Person

Here are some approaches that I developed from the Library of Life (real-world concepts from a real-world sales person). None fit neatly into any part of the sales process; however, they are important strategies for making the sale three-dimensionally. These ideas run the gamut from *how to organize your time to make more time for selling, how to implement creative personal marketing ideas, and how to perceive your customers.*

Get Organized

Now that you have this information floating around in your head about making calls, asking questions, listening, presenting, asking for the business, and following up, you need something else to make it work. **You need to get organized!** You will never make the calls if you do not have the time to make them. On her deathbed, Queen Elizabeth I said, "All my possessions for but one moment in time." Have you felt that way? You can never recapture a moment; once gone, it is gone! You can, however, organize yourself so that your time is used more wisely. Imagine what you could do with an extra hour a day! Perhaps, you would use it for study time. You could use the extra hour to make an extra sales call each day. If you averaged five sales calls a day, and increased it by one, at the end of the week, you made five additional calls. That translates to work-ing an extra day each week!

> **"If you spent just one hour a day studying any sub-ject, within five years, you could be a national expert in that subject."**   —Earl Nightingale

You might use the extra time to speak with existing cus-tomers to understand how they view your company and your service. You might use the extra time to work on long-term projects, those that you continually put off that must be com-pleted some day. Some more organized individuals use the time to plan: to plan their day, their week, their month, and their entire year. Imagine that scenario! You would certainly be a step ahead of your competition.

You could also use the extra hour to learn more about your company's operations to respond to those difficult client ques-tions that relate to how you can or cannot meet their requests. You could use the time to write personal notes to clients/prospects, to maintain your files, to set sales appoint-ments, or to spend more time with customers and prospects. Use the extra hour to follow up, to prospect, or better yet, to review the suggestions in this book. Just as in selling, learning is a process, not an event. Use your extra time to increase your knowledge of the sales process. These suggestions help you to better prioritize to find that extra hour each day.

Recently, I received a nice compliment from a woman who attended one of my seminars on organization. It was late after-noon as I visited with her sales manager, and the woman waved me into her office, "Joe, come see what I am doing! This is the best idea that I learned in your program. I am planning my sales for tomorrow!"

You might consider organizing your sales calls by territory to cut down on drive time. Often, sales people spend more time in automobiles riding around than they do making sales calls because they have not organized their drive time. When they do not organize their routes, they drive from one end of the city to the other, wasting time that could have been spent before a client.

To prove my point about how precious time is, close your eyes for fifteen seconds. (PAUSE) Guess what? You lost fifteen seconds of your life; it is gone forever! You will never get it back. Do not allow the precious seconds and minutes of your day to be taken up by non-productive activity. Think about an hourglass; the sand cannot be pushed back up the glass. The reality is that it is gone forever.

Do Not Wait—Do It Now!

Now what will waste your time more than anything? One word – PROCRASTINATION! So why do we procrastinate? It could be lack of planning, fear of success, a lack of skills, or maybe the task is just unpleasant. Did I say fear of success? You bet I did. In Dorothea Brande's book *Wake Up and Live* she writes that many of us have the will to fail because people show us sympathy when we fail. Some people would rather be failing for sympathy than succeeding for praise. The fact that success brings burdens does not help either. What do I mean by that? Win the lottery, and watch how many relatives call. Buy an expensive new car, and discover how far away you must park to avoid door dings. Buy an expensive new home, and more thieves will want to steal from you. Success brings burdens. But the burdens are only noticeable if you focus on them. Just remember that poverty also has its own set of burdens. At least, if you are successful, you can be comfortable while you experience your problems.

How do you overcome procrastination and get back on the road to success? Follow these ten steps:

❖ Chunk it down. We get mental indigestion from looking at a huge task. **Break your task down into small manageable pieces.** For example, a friend of mine kept telling me she was going to write a book, but after three years, she had not written the book. I told her to stop thinking about writing a whole book and to start writing a page a day. I told her to write one page a day for 250 days and she would have a book. She took my suggestion, and today she has a book.

❖ **Make an appointment with yourself to complete a task.** For example, at nine in the morning I am going to meet with me and write the first page of my book. Write the time on your calendar, and then show up for the appointment.

❖ **Set deadlines.** When I was in the advertising business, everything had a deadline. To set a reasonable deadline, determine what needs to be done and how long it will take. Begin with the due date or time.

❖ **Gather in advance the information that you need to complete a task.** *Here is how not to do it!* I sit down at my desk and realize that I need a pencil. I jump up to get a pencil. Minutes are wasted. I sit back down, and I need a dictionary. I get up again to look for the dictionary. I notice a James Michener book that I have not read yet. More minutes wasted. The more I leave my chair, the more I expose myself to the possibility of interruption. So, what do I do about it? Write a list of the things I need before I get started. Gather the items in one place and then begin.

❖ **Reward yourself for completing your task.** I used to buy myself a chocolate sundae after every good seminar. Five pounds later I decided to create a new reward idea. Only you know what motivates you. A new drum set motivated me. You may be motivated by a new outfit, or a ski jacket, or a set of tools. Choose your reward in proportion to the size of the task. For example, if you cleaned the basement, your reward might be a new book. But if you paint the whole house by yourself, your reward could be an expensive new watch. The watch would still be less expensive than hiring a painter.

❖ **Take mini-breaks.** Trying to work through a task without stopping is not wise. You will burn out quickly. When you feel yourself lagging, take a deep breath for eight counts, then exhale for eight counts, then stand up and stretch, reaching with your arms and legs, and trying to touch the ceiling with your hands. For a quick pick-me-up, rotate your wrist clockwise and counter-clockwise three times, then repeat with your ankles. This one is great for circulation. If you are on the phone for long periods, use a headset. Stand up and walk around the office instead of sitting in your chair. This will lift the energy in your voice when you speak to clients on the phone.

❖ You may have heard this one before but it is worth telling again and again. It is **a twenty-five thousand-dollar idea**. Ivy Lee, one of the great public relations gurus of the early twentieth century said to Charles Schwab, who was then president of Bethlehem Steel, "I have an idea for you. I will show you how to save time and make your company more effective." Schwab answered, "Whatever it is, I will try it and in six months, I will send you a check for whatever it is worth." Ivy went on, "Mr. Schwab, each day before you go home from work, write down the six most important things you *must* do tomorrow. Then number them in the order of importance one through six. Tomorrow morning when you get to the office, begin working on number one. Do not go on to number two until you are finished with number one." Schwab asked, "But what if I am interrupted while I am still working on number one?" Ivy replied, "You have to make a decision every time you are interrupted. Is the interruption more important than working on number one?" Charles put the idea to work and spread the system throughout his company. He liked it so much that he sent Ivy Lee a check for $25,000. You must decide what is more important to your success. If the interruption is a customer, the customer always comes first. If it is Bruce, who just wants to chat awhile, it is not that important. If your car is on fire, that is urgent. What happens if you do not complete all six things on your list today? Tomorrow number four becomes number one, and so on. So how do you keep track? Remember that little notebook I asked you to carry around for prospect information? Keep your to-do list there, or you may use a Franklin Planner, the Priority Management Planner, or a handheld computer. All are great tools to help you organize your time more efficiently.

❖ **Visualize the benefit of doing what you have been putting off.** Ask yourself, how am I going to benefit when this task is completed? For instance, because you did not procrastinate, you made those extra calls, and now you can see yourself cashing in your higher commission check. But why not visualize a step further? What are you going to do with the extra money you have earned? How about that fishing trip you have been dreaming about? See yourself standing in the stream as you cast, and see the fly floating in the air until it hits the water's surface. Now see yourself relaxing and waiting for the fish to bite. Imagine your excitement as you feel the line tighten, and the fish goes for your bait. See yourself pulling a five-pound trout from the water as it wiggles and fights to get free. Minutes later you are grinning as you hold your trophy up, and someone snaps a picture. That is what I mean by visualizing the benefit of doing a task. The benefit will move you to get the job done.

❖ **Mood follows action, action does not follow mood.** Here is an example. My wife Carol was frustrated with me because I had not pulled the weeds from our garden. I walked outside one day to get the newspaper, and I noticed that the weeds were really bad, so I bent down and pulled out one weed. Then I pulled out another weed, and then I got down on my knees and pulled another and another. In no time, I had weeded the entire garden. Why? Mood follows action. As soon as I began to weed, I was in the mood for weeding. So if you are putting off making sales calls, force yourself to make one sales call. Then make another. Suddenly, you will be in the mood. Consider it from another angle: Action does not follow mood; mood follows action.

❖ So, if none of the steps have worked, there is only one left. Nike came up with this one. Just do it! It is that simple. Three little words – **just do it!** Just make it happen. Take action. Think about it. Action is the opposite of procrastination. Use these ten ideas to accelerate your sales career, and procrastination will be a thing of the past.

If All Else Fails

Now that you have procrastination covered, there are other distractions that waste your time. Consider this analogy: if a person, who earns $30,000 a year, wastes one hour per day, he wastes $3,750 a year in wasted time? What could you do with $3,750? What eats up your time? Some obvious distractions are phone calls, casual conversation, shuffling and searching, putting out fires, responding to trivia, people, mail, meetings, and travel. You can eliminate some of the time-wasters and work more efficiently. If I visited your office today, would you be proud to have me there? When you enter your office, do you cringe at the mess on your desk?

Have you heard about the experiment where a scientist put an electrode on a sheep's leg, and when the sheep dozed off, it received a shock? The sheep was not allowed to relax, and consequently, in thirty days, the sheep developed ulcers. Every time you walk into your office and see your messy desk, you give yourself a jolt of tension and anxiety. So eliminate that grief from your life.

I have a system called the **stack-and-slash method** to eliminate mental clutter. Write these words on separate 3x5 cards and place them across the top of your desk, from left to right: DO. DELEGATE. READ. FILE. DUMP. Place the DUMP 3x5 card on the side of your desk and place a trashcan below the card. Put all the office clutter (books, magazines, memos, everything!) into one large stack in the center of your desk, and when the stack begins to teeter, start another stack. Go through each item to decide its fate. If it is an unwanted business card, drop it into the trashcan. If it is a project that you must do, place it beneath the DO card. If it is something to delegate, place the item beneath the DELEGATE card. Place any books to read beneath the READ card. You have essentially taken the large stack and converted it to small manageable stacks. Often, 80% of the items in the large stack end up in the trashcan, out of mind and out of sight. Remember that the objective of the stack-and-slash system is to organize the stacks according to tasks. Do not get sidetracked with an item in the stack that grabs your attention; continue until the job is completed. After completing the stack process, you ask what about the 20% that remains to be done? How do you eliminate the remaining clutter so that you can become mentally more productive?

You should have a stack of items under the card marked DO. Schedule a time on your calendar when you will complete each responsibility in the DO stack. The stack requires an action, or it will remain there forever. Keep track of your to-do tasks with an *daily* accordion file that contains slots for each day of the month. Place each responsibility on the day you plan to tackle it. If you plan to begin a task next month or upcoming months, place it in a *monthly* accordion file. For alphabetical reference, keep names, addresses, and important information on index cards, in a Rolodex, or on a handheld computer.

The DELEGATION stack is next. To determine what goes under DELEGATION, do the things that only you can do, then all else is delegated. Recently, I visited with a manager when her secretary interrupted our meeting to relate that a potential client called to request a meeting with a company representative. The manager stuffed the message into an over-stuffed calendar, and the following scenario ensued:

Joe: Whoa! What are you doing?

Manager: Well, I will get back with this guy.

Joe: How come? How many sales people do you have?

Manager: Four.

Joe: Four? If their job description is to sell, are they not the ones who should follow-up with potential clients?

Manager: Yes, but they are overburdened with too many accounts already.

Joe: Are you telling me that your sales people cannot handle any additional business?

What is the problem here? The manager decided to do everything herself and to ignore her own job description. If she is out of the office selling, she is not managing in the office. What about you? Are you taking on responsibilities that you can delegate to others? Are you selling or pushing paper?

To continue the story of the overzealous manager, I asked for a photocopy of a few forms before I left her, so she proceeded to photocopy the forms. When I reminded her that she had an assistant, she realized how often she had performed the tasks that others could do. Because the manager often assumed that everyone was busy, she habitually overburdened herself. Does this happen to you? As a manager, always consider if a task can be delegated to others. From time to time, read your job description to remind you to focus on your managerial duties.

What about reading materials? Put all magazines, articles, books, and other reading material under the card marked READ. You may wish to transfer your READ stack to a shelf or to a box. When you have something to read, put the item in your reading stack. Schedule a daily reading time to update yourself on your industry and to peruse the READ stack. Do not keep all your magazines just for the one article that you wish to read; clip the article and discard the magazine.

If it cannot be dumped, read, done, or delegated, it probably needs to be filed. Keep a file basket on your desk, and whenever you find something that needs to be filed, place it in the basket. Wait until the end of the day or the beginning of the next day to file, and if you have the luxury, delegate the filing.

Here are some additional time-saving tips. You, no doubt, have business cards from friends, associates, and sales representatives. Establish now that when you receive a business card, decide immediately where it gets filed. Input the information on your contact management software, or record it on a Rolodex. Purchase an electronic business card scanner, which scans cards directly into your computer system. Decide immediately whether the information is worth keeping or pitching.

To save time, answer mail on mail and memos on memos. When you receive a letter that demands an answer, write your response directly on the letter to return mail or fax. It will take half the time for a response, and you do not have to repeat the writer's request. Why not use voice mail or e-mail to your advantage? Think of voice mail as a delayed two-way conversation. When you make a call and hear voice mail, do not simply ask for a call back. What a waste of time! State your request clearly, and ask for the information you require. Your callers can then leave detailed answers to your questions when they return your call, especially if they get your voice mail. You may get all the information without speaking to the person. Impersonal though it is, it is efficient!

Sometimes friends and associates are our greatest detractors. Try using body language to discourage unwanted visitors to your office. I am not speaking of customers here, but about that office mate who invariably engages in long conversations, especially when you are working on your priorities. When the interruption enters your office, put your hand on the phone as if you are to make a phone call, look at your watch, and stand up. Do not be rude, but simply show them that you are busy.

How else can you take control of your time, instead of allowing others to control you? When swamped with interruptions, request quiet time. When I had my advertising agency, a creative director threatened to quit because he had no time to write ads. Whenever an account executive wanted an ad produced, he stopped the creative director to discuss it, whether it was convenient or not. Our solution was a directive that no one could speak with the creative director during certain hours, leaving ample time to communicate with him. At Bonura Business Development Group, the marketing director also understands this concept. If I interrupt her during phone times, she shows me the door! We understand the importance of this special time for her to market my engagements.

When you work with others, you constantly think of things to discuss with them. Keep running lists or a file folder for each person with whom you frequently communicate, and set a time to meet with them to discuss the items on the lists. If you have e-mail, use it to communicate detailed information. Ask the individuals to also keep a discussion list for you. Every six months, track your time for one week. Be honest with yourself when logging your time; analyze your time to eliminate the time-wasters.

Well, there it is. If you follow the advice, I guarantee that you will have an extra hour a day to reap the proven benefits of three-dimensional selling.

Be a Pig

By now, you should realize that three-dimensional selling involves more than knowing the basics. How do you set yourself apart from the competition? How do you approach the sales process from more than one angle? If it means tapping into your creative juices, show clients your creativity by sending more than a letter or brochure. I tried this on an industry association executive named Jim. I phoned him for a week, attempting to reach him and leaving fifteen messages for him! When I finally spoke with him, he brushed me off with, "Look, my desk is piled high with 200 brochures from speakers who want to speak at my convention. Just send your brochure, and I will review it." I knew that my chances to speak at his convention were remote unless I could creatively get his attention. I purchased a large, pink, ceramic piggybank, and I stuffed my proposal in the bank and sent the pig with a hammer and a note that read, *Inside this pig is the secret to helping your association members make more money in sales. Break me!* When I called a few days later and reached the secretary, she said Jim was busy. I told her that I was the guy that sent the pig. Her attitude changed, "You are the one who sent the pig? I will put you through to Jim!"

When Jim answered the phone I inquired about the pig. He said it was sitting there on his desk. I asked why he had not broken the bank, and he replied that it looked so good sitting on his desk that he decided to keep it. In fact, he said people were going in his office and putting money in the bank. I commented that he was already making money with me, and I had not yet spoken at his convention. Well, he had 200 applications and one pig. Guess who got the booking? I did! In the future, when you cannot reach someone, send something more than a brochure. Be creative. Send something three-dimensional.

It is a good idea to vary your contact methods with each client. If the first time you met them was in person, then the next time you might want to send a letter, then next try a fax or an article about their industry, then try e-mail. Thankfully, we are living in an age when there are many methods of communication. The variation keeps the client interested and eliminates the monotony of too many phone calls.

Whenever you complete work with a satisfied client, ask for a brief typewritten testimonial letter, including several areas that benefited their organization. When you receive the testimonial, fax it to hot prospects in that industry or send it to present clients to encourage additional engagements. With the testimonial, include a note that reads, "I knew that you would want to see this right away." This gives you an excuse to call to check that they received the fax. Faxing stresses immediacy, and it is one more positive way to get your name before the prospect/client. Do not hesitate to ask clients for testimonials because you can get most of your business from referrals.

When You Have To Put It In Writing

One area we have not covered is preparing creative proposals for prospective clients. You listened carefully to your prospect's needs during the questioning phase, and now it is time to design a creative proposal or presentation that customizes their needs, using the language of their industry. Avoid a stock solution if you have discussed their problems at length. Consider several approaches for the client. Can you partner with another business to give the client what he needs? Are you offering a long-term solution or a temporary band-aid? If you are offering a band-aid, how can you design a plan that will be more long-term? Basically, determine if the plan meets the needs of your client. Do not present a proposal simply because it is the cheapest one; *clients continue to do business with sales people who give them solutions.* Clients are not as concerned about price as they are about value.   If you can show them the return on their investment with you, you will establish a lifetime client.

> **Clients are not as concerned about price as they are about value.**

Pruning All The Branches

What about staying power with your client? If you want a long-term relationship with your client, get to know as many people as you can in the organization to assure your retention, should your contact leave. This is especially effective when you are dealing with a large corporation. *(I sometimes have twenty contacts with my larger clients.)* Another benefit is that you may find that you have opportunities in several areas of the company. Your primary decision-maker may be in Human Resources, but why not keep in touch with Sales and Marketing? Perhaps also Accounting? In this way, you will develop a broader sense of the company to solve problems based on more comprehensive company knowledge—a great way to keep your finger on the pulse of the company. Keep in touch with all your contacts; call them regularly. This assures that when you need the scoop on the latest merger or restructuring, they will not be strangers. Request to be included on the mailing list of the company newsletter. The more you know about them, the better it will be to serve them. If they have a Web site, check it occasionally to discover new developments.

Do Not Judge a Book By Its Cover

You know the old adage, "Do not judge a book by its cover." By the same token, do not pre-judge your customers. I visited a local car dealership when I discovered the importance of that maxim. In walked an old farmer, wearing dirty overalls and a straw hat that looked like something had taken a bite out of it. None of the car sales people wanted to serve the farmer, so they sent the new guy who was not excited either. As the new sales person approached the farmer, he asked how he could help the farmer. The farmer wanted to see a new truck, so the young man proceeded to show the farmer the low-line trucks, the cheaper models, but the farmer was interested only in the best model in the showroom. When the young man asked how the farmer would pay for it, the farmer reached into his pocket and pulled out a roll of bills and asked if cash would do. I wish you could have seen the look on the young man's face.

Each year when the farmer went to the tobacco auction, he came to town to also purchase a new truck. He did not have time to shop around for a truck. The young man misread his customer. The moral of the story is to treat all customers as if they have rolls of one-hundred-dollar bills in their pockets. Treat them well, not because they have the money, but because every customer deserves your respect. If you have treated people poorly because of appearances, remember Sam Walton drove a pick-up truck, and Howard Hughes dressed like a homeless person. If you treat every customer as if he is Bill Gates, who knows, maybe someday you will meet him, and better yet, do business with him.

Throwing the Rabbit

Put this smorgasbord of ideas to work for you by taking the time to see what needs to be done, learning how to do it, organizing the process, and then following through with action.

Chapter 15

Putting It All Together

Now I have a special bonus for you. You have learned many sales concepts, and perhaps you are wondering how to apply the concepts in the real world. In my seminars, participants enjoy my role play segments, so in this section of the book, I will pull together everything previously presented and apply it in one big role play. I will begin with the initial phone contact and end with getting the business. As you follow the role play, relate it to your product or service, mentally putting yourself in my role. Here is the scenario: I am a sales person with a commercial printing firm, selling services to an insurance corporation.

(phone ringing)

Receptionist: Good morning, Big Time Insurance, Pat Spinner's office.

Joe: Hello, this is Joe Bonura. You must be Pat's assistant?

Receptionist: Yes, I am.

Joe: And who is this?

Receptionist: This is Barbara Jones.

Joe: Barbara, I need your help.

Receptionist: Sure, how can I help you?

Joe: Well, what do we need to do for me to speak to Pat Spinner?

Receptionist: Well that depends. What company are you

with?

Joe: I am with BTS Printing, and I promised Pat's friend, Edgar Willis, that I would call her regarding a new image upgrade. I have some ideas that might save her some money and time. Does that make sense?

Receptionist: It just might. I know she has spoken with two printers; however, she is out of the office now.

Joe: What is the best time to reach her?

Receptionist: You can call back this afternoon at 3 o'clock, but if you like, you can leave a message.

Joe: No, I will be out of my office most of the day. Please tell her to expect my call around 3. Thanks for the help!

Receptionist: You are welcome, Mr. Bonura. Goodbye.

Joe: Goodbye.

(phone ringing at 3 pm)

Receptionist: Good afternoon, Pat Spinner's office, this is Barbara.

Joe: Hi, Barbara. This is Joe Bonura from BTS Printing again. Did I catch Pat in the office?

Receptionist: Sorry, Mr. Bonura, you just missed her. Give me your number, and I will relay the information to Pat.

Joe: Actually, my message is lengthy. To save time and writer's cramp, would you connect me to her voice mail?

Receptionist: Sure, I would be happy to.

(voice mail ringing): This is Pat Spinner. I am out of the office now, so leave your name, number, and a detailed message, and I will return your call as soon as possible. (beep)

Joe: Hello, Pat, this is Joe Bonura from BTS Printing. I promised your friend Edgar Willis that I would contact you regarding your new image upgrade. Edgar uses our printing services, and he is very happy with our work. I understand that you are looking to do a complete image overhaul. Perhaps, we can help, so I would like to learn more about what you would like to accomplish. You can reach me at 425-1795. If you reach my voice mail, just leave a time when I can return your call. Thank you.

(Later, phone ringing)

(voice mail picks up):

Hello, this is Joe Bonura. You have BTS Printing. I am out of the office, helping companies enhance their corporate profiles. Please leave your name, number, and the best time to reach you, and I will return your call promptly. Thank you. (beep)

Pat: Joe, this is Pat Spinner from Big Time Insurance. I am intrigued that you have done business with my friend Edgar; however, we are already talking with two other printers. If you like, you can try again tomorrow morning. I might be available then. Thanks.

(Next morning, phone ringing)

Receptionist: Good morning, Pat Spinner's office. This is Barbara.

Joe: Well, hello again, Barbara! This is Joe Bonura. Pat left a message that I could reach her at this time. Am I in luck?

Receptionist: Oh, I am sorry, Mr. Bonura, she was called out unexpectedly. May I take a message?

Joe: No, we keep missing each other. I have a better idea. Do you keep her calendar?

Receptionist: I sure do.

Joe: Then may I set a telephone appointment? Is she free this afternoon between 2 and 4?

Receptionist: Yes, she is.

Joe: How about penciling in 2 o'clock, and I promise I will call her at exactly that time. If you see a conflict before this afternoon, call me. Otherwise, I will assume that it is set.

Receptionist: All right.

Joe: Thanks for your help, Barbara.

Receptionist: No problem, Mr. Bonura. Goodbye.

(That afternoon, phone ringing)

Receptionist: Good afternoon, Pat Skinner's office. This is Barbara.

Joe: Hello, Barbara! This is Joe Bonura. Did it work?

Receptionist: It sure did! I will put you through to Pat.

(phone ringing)

Pat: Pat speaking.

Joe: Hi Pat, Joe Bonura.

Pat: Yes, Joe! I am impressed by your persistence; no one asks for a telephone appointment. When I told you that we were talking to two other printers, I did not expect to hear from you again.

Joe: Well, thanks. Telephone appointments save both time and phone tag. Edgar said you wanted to change your entire image. How come?

Pat: Well, we have had the same logo and out-of-date colors for 20 years. With the changes in the insurance industry, we want to look more friendly.

Joe: Friendly, huh? Why is that important to you?

Pat: It all started when one of our customers played golf with the president of our company, and he told the boss that our logo should have been put to rest with the dinosaurs. The next day the president asked me to do something about our image, so I called two printers.

Joe: I see. Other than the president's golfing buddy, did you do any research?

Pat: We sure did. We learned that many customers thought the same way. It is time to move into the twenty-first century. We want our customers and potential customers to know that we care. Our printed materials should reflect that.

Joe: What do you feel the immediate result of the change might be?

Pat: Well, we could attract a larger share of the younger, first-time buyers, and at the same time, we could cement our relationships with existing customers.

Joe: And what would that do for you?

Pat: (laughing) Well, we could pay for the printing!

Joe: Sounds good to me.

Pat: Seriously, our company growth is not as projected. We feel we have to do something to change that trend.

Joe: Well, what materials will you be changing first?

Pat: After new logo development, we will change letterhead, envelopes, business cards, and a new policy information package.

Joe: I see. Have you considered who will design your new logo?

Pat: I am not familiar with the experts in the graphics industry. I guess I will let my fingers do the walking in the yellow pages.

Joe: (laughing) Well, if it would help, I work with several good design studios in the city. May I send you the names and contacts of three I like best? You can interview them and make your selection. If that does not work, you can always go back to the yellow pages.

Pat: Oh, I would really appreciate that.

Joe: I will fax the names to you when we hang up. With a project like this, there is a lot I need to know. Let us set an in-person appointment so that I can ask you more about your project. I have some time on Wednesday afternoon, how about you?

Pat: Three o'clock is good for me.

Joe: Perfect, I will put it on my calendar. By the way, is there anyone else you will be consulting before you make the final decision?

Pat: The president and our VP of marketing will choose the logo development and artwork, and I have full autonomy to choose a printer.

Joe: Great! To maximize our time on Wednesday, can you send copies of current company materials? I will study them beforehand.

Pat: Sure! I will send them by courier this afternoon.

Joe: Great. Watch for my fax of the graphic design recommendations.

Pat: Will do.

Joe: See you Wednesday, Pat.

(Wednesday appointment)

Joe: Hello Pat. It is good to meet you in person. Hey, I noticed a light blue 1973 Chevrolet Caprice convertible parked in the spot with your name on it. Yours?

Pat: My pride and joy! I found it in the classifieds about 5 years ago, and I am restoring it a little at a time.

Joe: Makes me sorry that I sold mine.

Pat: You had one too?

Joe: Back in the 70's.

Pat: They are great in the spring, driving around with the top down.

Joe: It would have been, except mine was not a convertible. (laughing)

Pat: (laughing)

Joe: Shall we get started? I know you are busy.

Pat: You travel light; the last print salesman who was in here had three gigantic sample books and a packed briefcase. I almost fell asleep listening to him go over all his information.

Joe: I did not bring much with me because I want to first find out your needs. Here is my business card.

Pat: Serve person. That is a refreshing title.

Joe: I practice what it says. I am here to help you find solutions to your image changeover.

Pat: Great, I like what I am hearing already. Tell me about your printing company.

Joe: First I want to know more about *your* needs. You have given me an overview and the samples from the courier, but to be sure that we are on the right track, I need to get some more information. Tell me again what you hope to accomplish?

Pat: We are trying to develop a friendlier image through our printed materials: brochures, letterhead, maybe even a direct-mail campaign.

Joe: You also mentioned your information package on the phone.

Pat: Yes, that too.

Joe: So you are considering letterhead, envelopes, business cards, brochures, the information packet, and maybe a direct-mail campaign?

Pat: Yes.

Joe: Did you receive my fax on the graphics studios?

Pat: I did. By coincidence, our president knows the owner of one of them. Thanks for the input.

Joe: Did you decide to go with them?

Pat: As a matter of fact, we did. But not because he was a friend; they showed us an impressive portfolio. All your recommendations were good.

Joe: Glad to hear that. Your current president is Al Meyers, right?

Pat: How did you know that?

Joe: I checked out your internet site last week.

Pat: Impressive that you would check it out before visiting.

Joe: It helps to know your company better. What is your graphics company working on now?

Pat: Letterhead, envelopes, business cards, brochures and the information package. We are unsure about the direct-mail campaign.

Joe: How come?

Pat: It may be too expensive.

Joe: What makes you think that?

Pat: Printing and postage costs. We plan to mail to 300,000 current and potential customers.

Joe: What will be the purpose of the direct-mail piece?

Pat: To expose our new look.

Joe: If you eliminate the direct-mail piece, how else could you present your new look?

Pat: We have not really given it much thought. I guess now would be a good time to do that.

Joe: It could save you time and hassle at a later date. Besides image, do you want to generate new leads?

Pat: That is an idea. If we are already paying the freight to reach our clients and potential clients, it would make sense to make it do more than *look* good. Thanks for the suggestion!

Joe: And leads might help the direct-mail piece pay for itself.

Pat: I had not thought of that. Are you sure you are a printer? What is all this marketing advice?

Joe: You read my card; it says serve person. You were pleased with my graphics studio recommendations. Maybe I can suggest a mailing house, and you can check the postage and handling charges before you rule it out as too expensive.

Pat: Great, and what do you think about including a business reply card in the mailing?

Joe: Excellent idea! Just add it to your brochure as a perforated card. Have you thought about using four-color?

Pat: Not sure.

Joe: How come?

Pat: Cost!

Joe: Imagine that you did the mailing. On a mailing like this, the average return is about 2%, which translates to 6,000 leads. Add four-color, and you will increase your return to about 3.5%, which means about 10,500 leads.

Pat: That is almost double!

Joe: Correct. And to see if the mailing will pay for itself, calculate how many of those leads your sales people can turn into sales.

Pat: We can do that. We know our lead conversion rate.

Joe: Great! Combine your figures with the figures from the mailing house, and you will know the return on your investment.

Pat: Terrific!

Joe: Now your letterhead. Who will use it?

Pat: Everyone from Customer Service, to the sales people, to the president of the company.

Joe: Have you considered personalizing the letterhead for the president and some higher level executives?

Pat: Would that be complicated?

Joe: Not if you plan now. Do you think it would contribute to the friendly image that you are trying to convey?

Pat: It would add a personal touch.

Joe: Let your graphic studio know immediately to include it in their recommendations before you present the artwork to the president and the others.

Pat: Great idea!

Joe: I noticed that your old letterhead was yellowed over time. Since that is a sign of inferior paper stock, what are your thoughts on upgrading to a higher quality paper? Say, with a watermark?

Pat: I wanted to do that, but was concerned that watermark paper is expensive?

Joe: I guess you should consider that a watermark could contribute to the image you want to convey.

Pat: I am sure that it would give us a professional appearance.

Joe: And if your paper did not yellow over time?

Pat: We would ultimately save money because we would not have to throw it out.

Joe: Mention the watermarked paper to your design studio to include it in their cost estimate. How much letter-head to start?

Pat: At least 50,000.

Joe: Now if you decide to personalize some of it, as we discussed earlier, those quantities should be included in the quote.

Pat: OK. I will have an answer on that tomorrow.

Joe: In regard to the promotion kit, how do you feel about a gloss finish on the folder?

Pat: Do you have any samples?

Joe: I have one here.

Pat: I like the quality and the thickness.

Joe: You might like a folder with sealed pockets to hold all those policy pamphlets. How do you feel about that?

Pat: Glad you thought of it; there is so much to consider.

Joe: What quantity will you need?

Pat: 30,000.

Joe: Great! You can go two-color on the folder if you stay with a simple logo design.

Pat: All right.

Joe: What about envelopes and business cards? I need those quantities with a breakdown of the different names on the cards. When will the layouts be ready from the graphics studio?

Pat: They promised them by next Thursday.

Joe: And when do you think you will have a design

approved?

Pat: Hopefully by Friday morning.

Joe: I can quote as soon as I see what they propose. May I stop by next Friday afternoon to get the artwork and quantities you will need. Then, we can quote everything at once.

Pat: Thanks so much for your input, Joe. By the way, you have not told me anything about your printing company.

Joe: There will be plenty time for that on my next visit. When will you have numbers and layouts ready?

Pat: Call me next Wednesday, and we can arrange a time.

Joe: Thanks again for your time.

(Wednesday arrives)

Joe: Hi, Pat! Did everything go smoothly with the layouts?

Pat: We had a few changes, and the studio made them this morning and returned them in time to give them to you.

Joe: Great! I will return them by Monday.

Pat: Good, because one of the other printers had his secretary call to ask for the artwork to give a quote. I told him that he would have it by Monday. I have not heard from the third printer.

Joe: I am sure they will call, but right now I need to work on my quotes. I know the graphics studio has not provided a layout on the direct-mail piece, so I found a piece that is similar to your concept. It is four-color and it has a perforated return card. What do you think?

Pat: Yes, it is really on target. I mentioned your idea about the direct-mail piece to the president, and he said to pursue it. Since the mailing house will be here tomorrow, may I keep this piece to show them?

Joe: By all means. I have other samples at the office. The mailing house will need it to give you an idea of cost.

Pat: Thanks. You have been so helpful!

Joe: Glad to do it. See you Monday. Say about 10 am?

Pat: Can you make it for 10:30? The other printer will be here at 10.

Joe: Sure, 10:30 it is.

(Monday at 10:30am)

Joe: Hi, Pat. I see you are surviving this project.

Pat: Sometimes I wonder!

Joe: Since you asked last time, I would like to tell you about my company before we begin discussing your printing project.

Pat: We have been so busy talking about my needs that I have not given it much thought.

Joe: Even though we have been in the printing business for over 40 years, longevity does not always prove a company is successful. Can you think of some insurance companies that have been around a long time but they do not deliver?

Pat: I know a few.

Joe: That happens in every industry, Pat. We are a second-generation, family-owned printer, and we have not forgotten what made us successful. You, no doubt, have already noticed we do more than deliver pretty printed pieces.

Pat: Yes. You seem to be more solution-oriented. The other printer came this morning to pick up the artwork, and did not ask one question about my needs; he mumbled something about how I will like his pricing.

Joe: We both know that pricing is important; however, there are many factors that determine a successful relationship with our clients. There are three major factors in dealing with a printer. Compare it to a three-legged stool: if any of the legs are missing, the stool will collapse. We feel that a printer must be **on time, on target, and on budget.**

Pat: Right!

Joe: If your sales staff is ready for a mailing to hit the streets on a certain day, but the brochure is not ready when promised, what do you think might happen?

Pat: We would have many angry agents.

Joe: Yes. And what if the brochure hit the streets, and the printing quality did not reflect your professional image?

Pat: It would have been better to not mess with the mailing in the first place.

Joe: Yes. And, what if overruns and inaccurate estimates knock your budget out of whack?

Pat: Then I would be upset!

Joe: If this job were a failure because you choose the wrong printer, how would that reflect on your performance?

Pat: Since this whole thing was the president's idea, I would be a goner!

Joe: Before we look at the quote, Pat, please read a few letters from our satisfied customers. You already know Edgar, and you respect his opinion, and here are several business leaders who feel that we deliver what we promise. Feel free to pick up the phone and call any of them.

Pat: I especially like this comment from Mary Riley at Rainbow Professional Cleaning Services.

Joe: Yes, she had used two printers, based solely on price, but the price of not getting what she wanted was twice what it would have been had she gone with us in the first place.

Pat: Joe, I like what I see so far, but I must first do a cost comparison before I make a decision.

Joe: I would expect you to, Pat. Please realize in my quote that I have included a separate cost for each job to make it easy for you if you decide to eliminate one of the jobs.

Pat: I like that.

Joe: By the way, the direct-mail piece is reasonably priced. It should be lower than you expected.

Pat: Yes, a pleasant surprise. At this cost we can pay for the mailing and make a nice profit, even with a 3% return.

Joe: So it seems that you can do the mailing?

Pat: Yes, thanks for getting us to consider it in the first place.

Joe: My pleasure. I printed a sample of the new logo on the watermarked paper that your graphics studio recommended. I also printed a sample with the president's name to help you convince him to go with the personalized version. It looks great, don't you think?

Pat: It sure does! He will love it!

Joe: Here are some sample envelopes and business cards.

Pat: Thanks!

Joe: Well, Pat, you have seen our pricing and experienced our service attitude, what would need to exist to let us help you make this project a success?

Pat: I must see the quote from the other printer before I make a decision. I hope you understand?

Joe: Sure. When will you have the other quote?

Pat: By 10 am on Friday. I can call you around 11.

Joe: I will be visiting a nearby client at 10:30. I can stop by to get your decision.

Pat: I would not want you to go out of your way.

Joe: By now, Pat, you know how I feel about that. I will be here; it is no problem.

(Friday, around 11am)

Joe: Well, Pat, can we get started?

Pat: You missed your competition by 15 minutes.

Joe: I noticed. Is it a go?

Pat: I have not made my decision.

Joe: How come?

Pat: Well, his prices were 10% lower than yours. How can you help us on the price?

Joe: I can appreciate your concern about price, and I guess I did a poor job of convincing you that price is not the only factor in choosing a printer.

Pat: I think I heard you.

Joe: What exactly did you hear?

Pat: You said that being on time, on target, and on budget were important.

Joe: Correct. The question is how important are those factors to you?

Pat: Very important.

Joe: How come?

Pat: If the job were late and incorrect, it would cost more in the end. I would have egg on my face.

Joe: Then what else besides price would convince you that we would be the best choice?

Pat: You have demonstrated that you will go beyond what you see by recommending a graphics studio and a mailing house.

Joe: Of course, you can use them whether you go with us or not. I also want to assure you that our price is more of an investment than an expense. How would you feel, and how would the president feel, if you got the price you wanted, but delivery and quality were off-target?

Pat: Heads would roll! Namely mine.

Joe: Pat, are there insurance companies or policies that are less expensive than your company offers? That claim to offer the same benefits?

Pat: Yes, there are.

Joe: And what happens when an insured wants to make a claim from one of those companies?

Pat: They discover they are not covered.

Joe: Would you want to have the same thing happen to you on this printing job?

Pat: Right, Joe, I would not.

Joe: Have you spoken with any of my clients from the testimonial letters?

Pat: I spoke with two of the five, and they raved about you. They said you follow through on all of your promises.

Joe: Then can we help you remake your image?

Pat: Yes, you have earned it. We can work together on this project. Where do we begin?

Throwing the Rabbit

Substitute your product or service and put yourself in the role of the serve person in the above scenario.

Chapter 16

The Peace of Success

Although you have heard the maxim before, I cannot emphasize it enough, *"There is no gain without pain."* What is the opposite of pain? Peace! Yes, peace. Were you thinking of *pleasure*? What is pleasure if not being at peace? Whenever I ask a group of seminar participants what they want out of life and career, most say peace. How do you define this peace? As I sit here writing this book, I am listening to calm, relaxing music. I am at peace because I am doing two things I love to do: listening to music and thinking about sales.

The dictionary has two definitions for peace, the first being a state of mental or physical quiet or tranquility, calm. The second definition is a state of contentment after strife or conflict. I think the second definition describes the meaning of peace that I am thinking of.

In Joyce Meyers book, *Battlefield of the Mind*, she wrote about two artists who were asked to paint a picture depicting peace. One artist painted a quiet landscape of a lake far back in the mountains. The other artist painted a raging waterfall with a birch tree leaning out over the water, and a bird sleeping in a nest on one of the tree branches. The second picture describes peace best because there is no peace without opposition. It is the tearing of muscle during exercise that builds new muscle. It is the forest fire that renews the forest. It is the rejection in selling that teaches the right path. Rejection is pain, and there is no gain without pain. If you make an effort to do anything, there will be some degree of pain involved.

One year on vacation, my wife and I played golf for three days straight on Hilton Head Island. After three days of non-stop golf, we were experiencing so much pain that we needed a massage to work out those tight muscles. If the truth be known, we wanted to feel better so that we could play more golf in the remaining days of our vacation. The pleasure of playing more golf was greater than the pain of not playing golf in the remaining days of our trip. We should feel the same way about making sales calls. The pain of rejection cannot be as painful as sitting on the sidelines watching others drive nice cars, send their children to the best schools, live in beautiful homes, support their favorite charities, and take great vacations. For every reward in life, there is a price to be paid. A reward is a gift or prize for merit, service, or achievement. You do not have the right to succeed just because you exist. If you expect to receive the reward, you must pay the price of effort. When I played football as a youth, I hated practice and its endless drills, but it was the practice and the endless drills that enabled us to win the game. There is no gain without pain.

A reward is a gift or prize for merit, service, or achievement.

In one of my sales training seminars, a man reached into his pocket and pulled out a one-dollar bill. He asked me what it was, and I told him that it was obviously a one-dollar bill. To my surprise he said it was not. When he held it up to another class member, she said it was a buck. No again. The third person he asked was a little more creative in his answer when he replied that it was a one spot. Wrong. The man then held up the one-dollar bill, looked at the three of us, and said, **"It is a certificate of performance."** Wow! I had never thought of money that way before. What he was saying was that the better you perform, the more certificates you will have in your bank account and in your wallet. There is no gain without pain; you cannot separate the two. Look at your bank account now. For a sales person, the number of certificates that you have in that account is a good measure of the contribution that you have made to your financial success. It is also a measure of the amount of pain you have been willing to endure to get where you are in your sales career. If you are unhappy about your financial situation, only you can do something about it. Stop living as if you can step back and someone else will take care of you. Do you realize that you meet that same someone every morning when you look in the mirror. Ask yourself how much pain are you willing to endure to gain success and the peace that comes with it.

In this book, I presented the five principles that can lead you to a life of success and fulfillment in sales: Believe...Focus...Knowledge...Plan...Action. Remember to think about and practice the five empowering principles every day. Believe in God, believe in yourself, believe in your product, believe in your profession, and believe that you live in the most wonderful country in the world with opportunities that can exceed your wildest dreams. Focus on what you really want to achieve in life and in your career. If you do not know where you are going, then you have already arrived. In other words, always have something to live for and to move toward. Continue to learn and grow in your selling profession. Knowledge is not something you do only once in your lifetime; knowledge, like selling, is a never-ending process. Be a part of that process by learning something new every single day that can further your sales career.

If you do not know where you are going, then you have already arrived.

When you complete this book, write a plan of what you will accomplish in the next week, the next month, the next year, the next five years, and the next ten years. Think how each daily action will lead you to your ultimate destination, and be prepared to suffer the pain of taking that action. Each day make something happen. It is your responsibility to make the calls, ask the questions, listen to your prospects and customers, present solutions to their problems, look for the opportunity to serve them, and follow-up on a consistent and regular basis. Most importantly, remember that you are a serve person solving problems, and not a sales person pushing product.

When my wife was a young girl, she lived near a railroad crossing, and for the first few weeks, she remembered how the train's loud whistle and wheels clacking on the tracks woke the whole family in the middle of the night. After thirty days, the noisy train still passed but did not wake anyone. Why was that? Because her family had become accustomed to the noise, and it did not get their attention any longer. Life is the same way: great opportunities will come to us every day, but eventually our minds become numb to the possibilities that life presents. Hopefully, this book will be to you a wake-up call to do something different in your sales career. After a few weeks, you may no longer hear the whistle, and you may settle into the deep sleep of inaction. Challenge yourself every day to practice the information that you have learned. Allow this book to be a wake-up call in the middle of the night.

It is time for a new beginning in the world of three-dimensional selling. You can use the ideas in this book in the real world to sell more business. I hope that you have learned that three-dimensional selling is not about tricks or scripts; it is about relationships and about knowing your profession from the inside out.

Throwing the Rabbit

Wake up to the train in the night by taking a one-dollar bill and writing on the face of the bill "certificate of performance." Carry it with you and look at it every day to remind you of the reward at the end of the tunnel.

Chapter 17

You Have Their Whole World In Your Hands

I would like to close this book with a personal story. My daughter Ann and I had attended the 1994 National Speakers Association workshop in Charlotte, North Carolina. We were so excited about the workshop that we could not stop talking about it long enough to take a breath. We boarded Flight 632 at 6:30pm for the short flight from Charlotte to Louisville. We were talking so much that we did not realize that the plane had taken off. Because I am a private pilot, I noticed something wrong because the plane stopped climbing and leveled off. When I glanced at the passengers and fight attendants, no one seemed aware of anything unusual. The smiling flight attendants moved down the aisle taking our drink orders and distributing peanuts. So I ignored my imagined threat and returned to conversation with Ann. Suddenly, the pilot's voice confirmed my concern, "Ladies and gentlemen, we are having a problem with the landing gear. We will be back with you shortly."

Aware that I knew flight jargon, Ann asked me what was happening. I told her that it was probably an electrical failure, and they would flip the switch a few times and that usually took care of it. A woman sitting across the aisle heard my comments, so she asked what was happening. When Ann told her that I was a pilot, heads of all passengers nearby turned to my direction. I repeated to everyone how the pilot would attempt to recycle the gear by flipping the switch.

That explanation satisfied everyone until the pilot blared over the PA system two minutes later, "Ladies and gentlemen, we have tried recycling the gear several times unsuccessfully. We will be back in a moment."

Ten people turned to me with a what-happens-now look on their faces. Suddenly I was an expert on flight emergencies. I told them the co-pilot would probably try to retract and extend the gear manually as in the movie *Memphis Belle*. I assured them that manual extension of the gear generally works.

The pilot returned to the PA system and announced, "We attempted to operate the gear manually, and we can only get the main gear extended. The nose gear indicator light is showing that it is not down and locked. The flight attendants will prepare you for a crash landing." Now I do not know about you, but I always thought an airline would be a bit more sensitive when announcing the bad news! I guess he wanted to get our adrenaline flowing, just in case.

The flight attendants took their practiced positions in the aisle as their smiles faded to looks of concern. Over the years, I noticed that whenever flight attendants gave safety instructions before a flight, most of the passengers paid little attention. Not tonight. Everyone's attention was focused on the attendants, even when they reviewed the instructions for buckling and removing a seat belt. They asked the men to remove their ties and all sharp objects from their pockets, such as pens and pencils. They told the women to remove their high-heeled shoes. They warned us that smoke and fire might be a problem.

They pointed out the exit locations and floor lights leading to the doors. When they asked people sitting in the exit seats if they wanted to take the exit door responsibility, all four of them refused, but thank goodness for four big guys sitting behind us who were willing to take their places.

The pilot's voice pierced the tension that was building as he announced, "I will do a fly-by over the tower to see if the front landing gear is visible. While it would not guarantee that the gears locked, it is better than no gear at all. Do not worry though, folks, I have twenty years experience under my wing." His words had a calming effect, and it was reassuring to know he was thinking of us during this emergency. I was impressed with the professionalism and sensitivity of the flight attendants as they walked us through emergency procedures. Before they took their seats they explained how to maintain the crash position. The lights would be turned off two minutes before touch down so that our eyes could adjust to the dark. Just before they turned out the lights, I glanced at my daughter Ann. She had a tear running down her cheek. I thought of two things: she was the young mother of my three-year-old granddaughter who was waiting for her Mommy to return home, and she was my own newborn baby girl, being wheeled from the delivery room, with a pink ribbon in her hair and a tear running down her cheek. As the lights went out, we said I love you and prayed together for God's protection.

The pilot flew low past the tower. Although the gear was down, the tower could not tell if it was locked. In an attempt to jar the nose gear into a locked position, the pilot allowed the main landing gear to hit the ground for the first time. The plane bounced two feet off the ground and came back with a heavy thud. It skipped over the pavement, went down with another thud, and popped back up again. On the third time that the main gear hit the runway, it stuck, but the pilot held the nose gear up for what seemed like an eternity to dissipate speed. He very cautiously, as though landing on an eggshell, touched the nose wheel to the cement. The gear held, and the ordeal of Flight 632 was over.

All the passengers gave the captain and crew a standing ovation from a seated position.

I want to leave you with this. Customers expect your knowledge and professionalism to match that of the pilot of Flight 632. When we stepped on that plane, we expected the captain to know what he was doing. He knew how to use his controls, but he also knew how to control his environment. **He was a problem solver.** He looked at the emergency situation, and when one way did not work, he tried another. We trusted him with our lives. The pilot thought three-dimensionally and solved the problem.

When customers do business with you, they trust you with their money. A customer depends on you to see and understand all the dimensions of his or her investment. He expects you to take his/her investment to a safe and happy landing. **Remember this in selling – keep the main thing, the customer, the main thing.**

When you put relationships first, all else will fall into place.

When you serve the needs of others, you are nourishing relationships and your sales career. Make it an awesome day, every day! Serve someone.

Throwing the Rabbit

Throw the Rabbit one last time by making an action plan of how you will assimilate and implement the sales success principles that you have learned in this book.

194

Action Plan

_____
_____
_____
_____
_____
_____
_____
_____
_____
_____
_____
_____
_____
_____
_____
_____
_____
_____
_____
_____
_____
_____
_____
_____
_____
_____
_____
_____

Action Plan

_____
_____
_____
_____
_____
_____
_____
_____
_____
_____
_____
_____
_____
_____
_____
_____
_____
_____
_____
_____
_____
_____
_____
_____

196

Action Plan

_____

_____

_____

_____

_____

_____

_____

_____

_____

_____

_____

_____

_____

_____

_____

_____

_____

_____

_____

_____

_____

_____

_____

_____

Action Plan

_____
_____
_____
_____
_____
_____
_____
_____
_____
_____
_____
_____
_____
_____
_____
_____
_____
_____
_____
_____
_____
_____
_____
_____
_____
_____
_____

Put Joe's "Knows" In Your Sales Career

Joe Bonura works with business leaders and individuals who want to grow. He is known as a "real world" speaker, author, and consultant who gives his audiences easy-to-do, high-impact ideas they can apply immediately to increase sales, turn customer satisfaction into customer excitement, and to develop personal life skills.

His background is unique. Joe owned and operated a highly successful advertising agency for 17 years. During that time, he found his advertising campaigns were more effective when he trained his clients to sell and to better service their customers. As word spread that Joe was a quality consultant and speaker, companies throughout the world asked him to help turbo-charge their people and their businesses. When the demand became so great, he sold his agency to start his own speaking and consulting firm, Joe Bonura & Associates, Inc. Since then, hundreds of companies and thousands of people from London to the Philippines and all fifty states have heard and benefited from Joe's powerful success system.

He is author of the audio learning systems, ***Three-Dimensional Selling©***, and ***Turning Customer Satisfaction into Customer Excitement©***. He presently serves on the Board of The National Speakers Association.

Joe Bonura, CSP (Certified Speaking Professional)
President, Joe Bonura & Associates, Inc.
Call 800-444-3340
http://www.bonura.com

To order additional copies of this title,
call 800-444-3340 or visit
website: www.bonura.com